The Emotional Dashboard

How to find peace in a world of crazy

Doe Kopp

Copyright © 2023 by Doreen Kopp [a.k.a. Doe Kopp]

With contributions by Dwight Kopp

Cover photo by Craig Adderley

All rights reserved.

No portion of this book may be reproduced in any form without written permission from the publisher or author, except as permitted by U.S. copyright law.

Some peoples' names have been changed to protect their privacy.

All Scripture is taken from the Amplified Bible.

Contents

Foreword	1
Preface	3
PART ONE	7
1. The Life of Fred	9
2. Journey to Life	13
3. In the Vine	19
4. Squatters	25
5. Oppression	31
6. Emotional Dashboard	35
7. Early Warning System	41
8. Roots and Fruits	47
9. Flashing Lights	51
10. Forgiveness	59
11. Forgive, Repent, Receive	65
12. Sentry Duty	73

PART TWO	77
13. Disappointments	78
14. A Question of Character	82
15. Divided Heart	87
16. Overcomers	95
17. Sons or Orphans	99
18. Trauma	103
19. Perfect Peace	110
20. Dashboard Mentality	115
APPENDIX A	117
APPENDIX B	119
APPENDIX C	123
Acknowledgments	131

Foreword

"But I tell you the truth, it is to your advantage that I go away; for if I do not go away, the Helper (Comforter, Advocate, Intercessor - Counselor, Strengthener, Standby) will not come to you;" (John 16:7, AMP)

Like many Christians, I have often wondered with amazement at what it would have been like to walk side by side with Jesus during His time on the earth. I cannot imagine anything more remarkable. And yet, Jesus tells His disciples that walking in fellowship with the Holy Spirit is *even better* than walking in person with Him. This absolutely astonishes me.

I believe many of us fail to experience this fellowship. The Holy Spirit isn't a second-best option. Jesus tells us, "But when He, the Spirit of Truth, comes, He will guide you into all truth [full and complete] truth." (John 16:13)

The Holy Spirit is here to give understanding and revelation. We can trust Him, because He speaks what He hears, and what He hears comes directly from the Father. All too often in today's church we discount or disregard the role of the Holy Spirit in our daily lives and miss out on the victorious life Jesus came to give us.

We hesitate to seek or listen for the voice of the Holy Spirit because we lack trust in our own discernment. Just because we might misinterpret or struggle to know the difference between the Spirit's prompting and our own flesh does not mean we should shut Him out. That is the opposite of Jesus' instructions!

Discernment comes from God. He will grant it when we come before Him, humble and with pure intentions. And ... He is a God of grace. There is room for mistakes. Our God is good and perfect, and will not leave us floundering in error.

In the chapters that follow, we will discover how to seek the Spirit's help to achieve the victorious and abundant life God promised.

We are not left to figure this out on our own. The Holy Spirit guides us into a new way of thinking, a new way of living, so we may experience the abundant life God intended.

- Nicole Brandt

Preface

Many years ago God sent Jenna to us (not her real name). She had endured unimaginable abuse during childhood. God told her to ask us to pray for her inner healing. We knew this was what God wanted, but we had no idea what we were doing.

Jenna's trauma went deep. We were in way over our heads. With cliff notes from a friend, we plunged in constantly asking Holy Spirit, "What do we do here?"

And the Holy Spirit answered. Step by step, He unwrapped the dirty bandages around her heart and poured healing in. During our second meeting, she said, "Already, I've gotten more healing than thirteen years of therapy!" We were privileged to have a ringside seat as Jesus brought His daughter back to life.

After praying with countless people over 20 years, the general response has been the same.

If there is one thing to learn here, it is this: **Ask Holy Spirit, then expect Him to answer.** Let me be clear: we aren't the answer people. We are not the healers. This isn't a magic formula. It's all about Him. Holy Spirit is the Counselor who guides us into all truth (John 16:13a).

We applied what we learned to our own lives and family and have seen profound healing. Besides being a defining point in our spiritual growth, it has become a lifestyle of discipleship that we want to pass on. Jenna's testimony planted the seeds for this book.

This isn't "special" knowledge for leaders or ministers. This is for all the frustrated, hungry and thirsty. This is for the captives who yearn for freedom but have given up because it seems impossible.

Dwight and I have since received training from multiple inner-healing ministries, all of which confirmed what the Holy Spirit taught us from the beginning.

By repenting of our broken understanding of who the Father is we invite an encounter with Truth that heals and reconnects us to Him.

This book is for those who've run out of willpower to keep all the rules. This book is for those who desire to live righteously but come up short. It's for those who have tried to think all the right thoughts, knuckle under and get their act together yet are overtaken time and time again by fear, addiction, insecurity, anger, and hopelessness.

If you've found behavior management, self-will, rule-keeping and pretend to be stressful and exhausting, this book is for you. If you're tired of accountability partners asking questions about your latest failure and the guilt-assisted spiral of condemnation and self-hatred, keep reading. If your heart has shut down, gone numb and lost hope, keep reading.

If you're tired of living with a broken heart, you're in just the right place.

Jeremiah 6:16, "Thus says the Lord, 'Stand by the roads and look; ask for the ancient paths, where the good way is; then walk in it, and you will find rest for your souls.'"

PART ONE

Emotions and Core Beliefs

The Life of Fred

Fred, the minivan, became part of our lives in 2003 when we moved back to the United States after living in Zambia for 18 months. In Africa we had owned a Nissan Safari, outfitted for our life in the bush (wilderness). The Safari was Dwight's dream, adventure vehicle complete with roof-top gas jerry cans, a machete and axe in back, and a winch which we actually needed on occasion to get through the roads.

Moving back to the mini-van-driving United States where off-roading is generally discouraged was a major comedown. Not only did Dwight want a Nissan Safari, he wanted to NEED a Nissan Safari.

But I was telling this story about Fred. Already he had one mark against him for being a minivan. The second mark against Fred was that half of America owned a green Fred minivan. We aren't fans of the 'bandwagon.' We prefer to make our own trails.

We bought Fred on the recommendation of a friend who

found him at an auction. Since we needed to make a thousand mile road trip with three young children and one on the way, Dwight made an impulse warranty purchase. The warranty was good for 3,000 miles or three months, whichever came first.

The thousand mile road trip went just fine. But while driving to a local park, Fred threw an engine connecting rod. We needed a whole new engine just 97 miles short of the warranty limit! So suspicious was this that the insurance company sent an agent to investigate. Thankfully, they paid for a new engine. We were good again.

But that was not the end of Fred's story.

Soon afterward, Fred's front, right hubcap fell off. We pulled over and fished it out of a corn field. Dwight thumped it back on.

Driving down a highway it came off again. We ordered a new one.

That came off, too. Then we noticed that 75% of green Fred minivans were missing the same hubcap. What is it with that? Without a hub cap, the front, right wheel looked friendless and unloved. Still, we didn't bother putting it back on.

Gradually, other issues cropped up. Fred's windows would get stuck. Usually down. The seats got wet; we got cold. When they would cooperate and go up again, we made a new rule: Do NOT put the windows down! Seemed like an easy fix.

Have you ever pulled up to a drive-thru with a window that doesn't go down? Do you know how awkward it is to pull past the drive-thru toll booth, bank window or fast food speaker, open the door and have to get out to use it?! Other drivers loved being stuck in my line at the toll booth. These were the days before EZ Pass.

Then the interior lights wouldn't go off. The next morning, with places to go and things to do, we were greeted with a dead battery. So Dwight unplugged that fuse. Not having interior lights is a minor annoyance until you are traveling with small children at night.

The speedometer lied. Ask Dwight how he found out about that. Police officers do not like to be surprised by a driver who gets out of the car to greet them. They like you to open your window.

Then the rubber seal around the side door began to creep out of place. It acted like a brake for the sliding door. One of the big kids had to sit low in the back seat and kick the door with all their strength to close said door.

Wait. There's more.

Personal favorite: Fred developed a ding. Not a dent — that would have been easy to ignore. Fred's high pitched ding-ding-ding-ding-ding sounded any time our speed dropped to less than 20 mph. Concentrating on the road in heavy traffic while Fred was dinging away and children asked questions in the back seat was like doing a calculus problem with a soprano duck pecking at your ear drums.

But the straw that broke the camel's back happened five miles from home after a beach vacation.

Fred needed gas.

THE EMOTIONAL DASHBOARD

Dwight got out to pump and as he shut the driver's door, it bounced back at him. It sounded like a metal pipe was stuck between the door and the car. Fred had locked himself open. Crash, bang, crash, bang, crash, bang.

How does one drive a vehicle while holding the door shut? You don't. You stretch a bungy cord from the driver to the passenger door. But every time we turned right, the door yawned open and crashed shut again.

Humiliations galore.

Fred had so many issues that his dashboard lit up like a city skyline. When Fred's check-engine light came on, we thought the safe thing to do was have him checked. The mechanic determined the engine was fine, but Fred's computer something-something had gone squirrelly. At least the engine didn't need to be replaced again. Is it better to have a sound engine with no warning lights, or a bad engine with a reliable warning system?

Fortunately, our emotions serve as a dashboard warning system, so we can know when our heart is in distress. The warning lights are not the problem. They merely indicate a deeper issue. If we don't pay attention to our dashboard, we run the risk of bigger problems.

Emotions are a gift to help us decode buried hurts, unforgiveness or trauma. When we bring these to God for His healing, He refreshes and restores our souls.

Journey to Life

We all want to be whole and authentic. Everyone wants the jumbled mess of their life to be put right. In vain, we try to fix our brokenness with behavior modification by carefully monitoring our actions or reactions. At best, this only covers wounds and offers a pretend version of ourselves. The heart remains broken and hidden behind the facade that everything is okay.

How then do we find our way to authenticity and wholeness?

Emotions are a God given portal to our hearts where core beliefs reside. Negative emotions reveal where we believe lies about God. What we believe about God, life, others and ourselves drives our emotions and behaviors. Beliefs, emotions and behaviors are inseparably connected.

Beliefs drive emotions. Emotions drive behaviors. Every. Single. Time.

THE EMOTIONAL DASHBOARD

FOR EXAMPLE:
GOD WASN'T THERE FOR ME → ABANDONMENT, FEAR, ANGER → REBELLION: I WILL TAKE CARE OF MYSELF

Lies and wrong beliefs about God poison our heart against Him. This poison seeps into other areas of our lives, affecting our minds, bodies, emotions and behaviors. When we deal with the lies and false beliefs about God, ourselves and the world, we cleanse the poison. By replacing the lies with truth, we bring healing, life, righteousness and blessing to our lives. We will never be able to walk in freedom, life and peace without first dealing with underlying beliefs that have caused the broken mess inside.

If you are tired of the brokenness, trauma, pretend, the busyness and addictions to escape the inner pain, there is another way. There is hope. Father mends our hearts and gives us the power to live holy lives. This journey is a lifestyle; a way of inviting God to clear the springs of your heart so you can find inner rest in His joy, peace and wholeness.

The Holy Spirit leads us into all truth. "And you will know the truth ... and the truth will set you free," (John 8:32). Understanding the truth about the Father's love heals our hearts and sets us free.

"Now on the last and most important day of the feast, Jesus stood and called out [in an loud voice], 'If anyone is thirsty, let him come to Me and drink! He who believes in Me [who adheres to, trusts in, and relies on Me], as the Scripture has said, 'From his innermost being will flow *continually* rivers of living water.'" John 7: 37-38

If we aren't experiencing ever-increasing levels of love, joy, peace, patience, kindness, goodness, faithfulness, gentleness and self-control, then we aren't walking in truth. We cannot muster them up. Redemptive discipleship happens at a heart level. As we bring the light of truth to dark places, we bring the kingdom of heaven to our heart. We can't bring the kingdom of heaven to anyone else if we haven't got hold of it first.

Here's how it works: Pain and turmoil are the dash lights inviting us deeper. What will you do with it? You can allow your emotions to lead you higher, toward healing and truth. Or you can let them take you in a downward spiral.

THE EMOTIONAL DASHBOARD

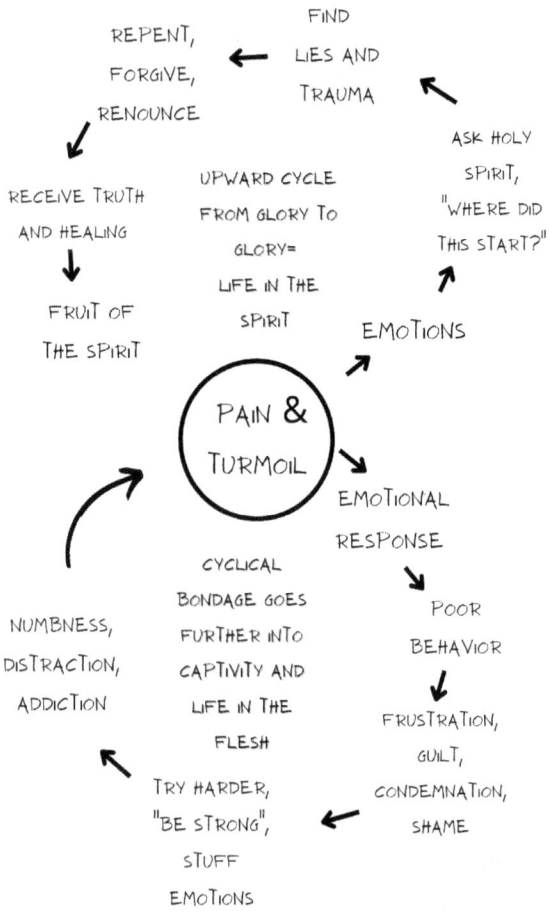

Cycle of pain and turmoil: Choose your own ending.

The grace to walk in the fruit of the Spirit is evidence that our core beliefs are in line with truth. The converse is also true. "Every healthy tree bears good fruit, but the unhealthy tree bears bad fruit. A good tree cannot bear bad fruit, nor can a bad tree bear good fruit." Matthew 7:17-18. In any given moment, are you inhabited by peace, joy, rest (positive emotions and responses) or turmoil, stress, anger, impatience or agitation (negative emotions and responses)? **Fruit is always the litmus test.**

In the Vine

Like most people, your alarm probably goes off before you're done sleeping. You heave yourself out of that comfy place and stare dumbly into the closet, vainly hoping for inspiration. You put it on anyway. The morning drill includes a desperate grab for mediocre coffee and a microwaved waffle that's tough in the middle.

You nag the kids with the daily hurry-up-or-you'll-be-late song while listening to fragments of the day's headlines— just enough to confirm that the world is still a disaster before you plunge into your weekday chaos.

True to form, you leave two minutes late because you can't find your keys and get stuck BEHIND the world's slowest school bus along your entire route to the office.

You rush all morning to make it to a job you don't like, to work with people you didn't pick, to get a too-small paycheck that only covers the really boring bills.

By the time you run the routine in reverse at day's end, you're spent, grumpy, and disjointed. You stumble through the evening drill of supper, homework and baths and stare longingly toward nine o'clock when the kids go to bed. Finally, you grab a glass of wine and crash in front of the television for a long, mind-numbing escape.

After all, we deserve a survivor's reward: (another) glass of wine, a bowl of ice-cream or a micro-binge of our favorite reality show. But this relentless diet leaves us malnourished and spiritually bankrupt.

The twenty-first century has given us much in the way of technology and advancements. However, we are less in touch with our hearts, and more disconnected from each other than ever before. Cell phones may link us technologically to the whole world, but they have enabled us to avoid authenticity. Escape from present reality feels good, but only temporarily. Eventually exhaustion or burn out will catch up with us.

Rather than eye contact, hugs and the undivided attention of face to face relationships, we have distraction, interruption, information and entertainment. This fast-paced culture has left us too busy and overwhelmed to enjoy time alone. We desperately need space to be quiet, to contemplate, to listen to our hearts and to Father God. Connection to the Father is our biggest loss—His Spirit in us, His wisdom, help, comfort, and truth. If we don't nurture our spirit and our relationship with the Holy Spirit, we miss out on this most meaningful connection.

There is a profound difference between escape and refreshment. Escape seeks to run, hide, or cover the cry of our heart. But the pressure will not just go away. By turning to the

Life-Giver, we reenergize and replenish the whole person.

"But Jesus Himself would often slip away to the wilderness and pray [in seclusion]." (Luke 5:16)

True rest requires that we refresh our spirit. One of the primary functions of our spirit (besides connection to the Holy Spirit) is to nurture our whole self. When the spirit is rejuvenated, our soul/body can receive health, hope and joy to keep going. **Our spirit is like our life-line to the Father.** For long-term health and restoration we must nurture this forgotten yet vital connection to the Holy Spirit.

Jesus said, "I tell you the truth, it is to your advantage that I go away, for if I do not go away, the Helper (Comforter, Advocate, Intercessor - Counselor, Strengthener, Standby) will not come to you; but if I go, I will send Him (the Holy Spirit) to you [to be in close fellowship with you]." (John 16:7)

Yes! Jesus said it is "to our advantage" that He left, so that we could have the Holy Spirit. The Holy Spirit surpasses Jesus on earth. Why? The Holy Spirit lives in each of us, always empowering us to live like Jesus did. Jesus lived in constant communion with the Father through the Spirit.

Jesus did not say He would leave us with the Bible. If that was the most important gift we needed for spiritual growth, He would have mentioned it. But Jesus made it a point to tell us about the Holy Spirit. The Holy Spirit gives us ALL we need to know the Father. The Word of God is very important! But it isn't the MOST important gift Jesus gave us.

Before you call me heretic and throw this book in the fire, consider that we live in a very privileged time. For thousands of years, due to lack of printing presses, illiteracy, language barriers and persecution, few people had access to Scriptures, let alone a personal copy. Yet Christ built His church. Even today we see this in China, Russia, Iran, Iraq. The members of the Godhead are not Father, Son and Holy Scriptures, but Father, Son and Holy Spirit. Sadly, we often give the Holy Spirit the backseat to the Book. The Bible is living and active BECAUSE of the Holy Spirit.

In the Holy Spirit, God promises us "[absolutely] everything necessary for [a dynamic spiritual] life and godliness, through true and personal knowledge of him." (2 Peter 1:3)

We are called to an inner, emotional strength by which we have the capacity to love those around us even when they push all our buttons. We are called to walk in the fruit of the Spirit and not blow our cool with family, co-workers or the jerk driver who cuts you off then gives *you* the finger.

We've all blown it. Welcome to the club. And while we do need to clean up our messes, 'blowing it' creates an opportunity to take a hard look at our connection to the Vine.

If we need to manage or manipulate situations (or people) in order to display love, joy, peace, patience and self-control, that is not the fruit of the Spirit. True spiritual strength comes from God and has the *super-natural* capacity to produce good fruit no matter what life throws our way.

This is neither a condemnation session, nor a fake-it-til-you-make-it solution. It's not about having the right carrot to look forward to on the weekend, or the correct balance of circumstances so you can push through.

Without His companionship to refresh us, anything else is a band-aid on a broken arm. We need to hear His encouragement daily. We need His joy in the hard moments, His affirmation, wisdom, and hope. In short, **He is our Source of Life**.

Technology and entertainment aren't evil. The danger comes when we use them to mask a need they can neither identify nor satisfy. Make time to step away to reconnect with Holy Spirit.

"Why do you spend money for that which is not bread, and your earnings for what does not satisfy? Listen carefully to Me, and eat what is good, and let your soul delight in abundance. Incline your ear [to listen] and come to Me; Hear, so that your soul may live; and I will make an everlasting covenant with you." (Isaiah 55:2-3)

The spiritual disciplines (silence, solitude, fasting, prayer, and meditation) create space for Holy Spirit to identify the flashing lights on our emotional dashboard. Together they provide a tangible way to nurture an intimate relationship with God - welcoming His Presence into our innermost places. Being in Father's Presence strengthens our spirit. Nurturing our spirit strengthens our whole self.

God is Truth. Truth sets us free. Freedom gives life.

We need to eat daily to sustain our physical bodies. It is no different with the spiritual. Don't let the battery or the gas tank get to the lowest level before refilling. The regular practice of inner recalibration brings true strength, wholeness and peace.

"Remain in Me and I [will remain] in you. Just as no branch can bear fruit by itself without remaining in the vine, neither can you [bear fruit, producing evidence of your faith], unless you remain in me." (John 15:4)

Squatters

According to real estate law in our state, it is possible for a squatter to gain legal title to my land. If a trespasser inhabits land openly and the owner fails to exercise the legal right to evict him, eventually the trespasser can sue for title. In short, the encroacher can become the new land owner. When that happens, even the courts recognize the squatter as having legal authority over that territory.

This law of real estate is reflective of the spiritual legal system. We may have title to land, but we must also exercise the rights and responsibilities that go along with the legal title. If we invite the enemy or ignore his trespass in our heart, we have failed to exercise our authority as stewards of God's property.

Simply put, **what we don't actively forbid, we allow**.

For example, if I make agreements (actively or passively) with the lie that I'm alone, then I unwittingly allow the demonic rights to my property. The emotional result of this lie might be fear, insecurity or dread.

When Dwight, my husband, was five years old, he was sent to boarding school. Where he lived in Central Africa, boarding school was considered a step up from sending children overseas for school. But a five-year-old has a hard time seeing three-month terms away from home as an improvement. Even though he knew his parents loved him, he felt abandoned. The enemy used that trauma to whisper the lie that he was alone. And in parts of his heart, he believed it. (Read Dwight's story in his book Made In Africa, available on Amazon.)

Long after leaving boarding school, the lie remained as a squatter in his heart. The truth of God's nearby-ness seemed disconnected from reality. Because Dwight buried his trauma, he never dealt with the lies and the squatter was allowed to stay. From that position, the enemy held legal rights to exercise influence in Dwight's life. Because of that stronghold, fear, insecurity and dread plagued his life.

This 'partnership' created a legal agreement the enemy could exploit to increase his influence (fear). Any place we "partner" with the enemy (actively or passively) by believing lies about God, ourselves or others, we give away 'real estate' to the enemy. The Bible refers to this as a 'stronghold.'

It isn't a metaphor; it is a spiritual reality.

When a person makes an active or passive agreement with the enemy, he opens a doorway that allows the demonic to enter and exercise legal authority in his mind, body, thoughts, will, desires, emotions or relationships.

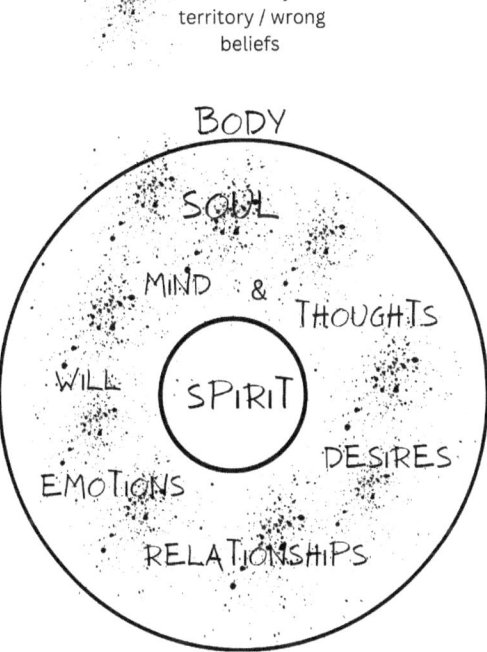

The enemy can't exercise dominion except where we have given away authority.

The implication here is sobering. Christ rescued us into His Kingdom, our "Promised Land." But just like the Israelites, we have to take dominion over our land and exercise the legal authority Christ gave us in order to possess it. There are still enemies to be evicted.

God is saying, "Stand up! Look around you! The cross restored your authority to take possession of your inheritance. Repent of any place where you have abdicated that authority. I paid the ultimate price to buy it back. It's yours if you'll take it!"

"Hear, O Israel! The Lord is our God, the Lord is one [the only

God]! You shall love the Lord your God with all your **heart** and **mind** and with all your **soul** and with all your **strength** [your entire being]." (Deuteronomy 6:4-5)

So often, especially for those of us raised in church, we know the truth in our heads, but our hearts don't get it. This is where lies are still at work in our emotions, desires, will, etc. Quoting Scripture in this case is like planting seeds before pulling the weeds. Most seeds will not sprout, and those that do, will struggle to survive. We must clear the weeds before planting the seeds.

The heart needs healing and truth in order for the whole person to experience freedom, life and peace. Pain and loss need to be recognized and grieved. Offense and bitterness must be laid down before the heart will experience the Father's love. We don't have a right to understand why certain things happen. Let go of understanding and choose to trust Him as an act of your will. Holding on to offense creates walls that prevent relationship with our Father. When we love God with all our being, we choose to trust every area of our life to Him. As we do, He heals, restores and redeems from the inside out, causing rivers of living water to flow. Clean refreshing water provides life, joy and hope for everyone.

"Therefore, since we have these [great and wonderful] promises, beloved, let us cleanse ourselves from everything that contaminates body and spirit, completing holiness [living a consecrated life - a life set apart for God's purpose] in the fear of God." 2 Corinthians 7:1

Disclaimer: The body/soul/spirit diagram is for understanding only, not for theological purposes. The spirit, soul and body are not separate, but closely intertwined. Everything one experiences, impacts the other. There is no segregation of spiritual, emotion or physical. Whatever touches the body, touches spirit. Therefore, all decisions, emotions, thoughts and actions affect our whole being.

Oppression

Though we are inhabited by the Holy Spirit, where we do not surrender the mind, thoughts, will, emotions, desires, relationships or body to God, the demonic realm can still harass or oppress us.

What does harassment look like? All of us have spent a night tossing and turning with guilt, fear, worry, confusion, you name it. That relentless head noise or feeling of shame is demonic harassment. Demons (and their lies) make us feel harassed, heavy, hopeless or ashamed. God's voice brings hope, encouragement, life, and peace. While Holy Spirit convicts us of wrongs, He does so with hope and encouragement for change.

At times, the lack of peace may manifest as low level stress or irritability, intolerance of noise, crowds and activity. Or it could be the opposite; a driving restlessness, distraction or need to escape the quiet. Inner mental or emotional turmoil just leaves you feeling "off". Avoidance tactics only prolong the misery. When you pay attention to the feelings or plaguing thoughts and bring them to God for adjustment, you will realize how sweet His redemption is. No longer will you want to tolerate the turmoil that you once thought was normal.

I've learned to recognize symptoms of harassment; I restlessly run my fingers through my hair or continually roll over in bed to "get away" from the voice that's chasing me. Every person has their own tells.

Elizabeth (not her real name) came to us with a disturbing dream. "I woke up from a nightmare where I was being chased," she said, "but the most chilling part was that I woke up with my teeth bared, and I was growling. Out loud. That freaked me out. Why was I snarling?"

It seemed obvious the snarling was demonic. Knowing the demonic only has authority where permission is given, we asked the Holy Spirit to reveal the agreements and the reasons for them. We knew from previous conversations that Elizabeth had faced abuse as a child.

Animals snarl as a warning to trespassers. It made sense then, that in this dream, Elizabeth was re-experiencing childhood abuse and God was revealing her agreement with the demonic realm that needed to be dealt with in order for her to experience peace and life.

The Holy Spirit used a dream to reveal agreements Elizabeth made in childhood that still held her hostage as an adult. Elizabeth's growling portrayed her emotional and physical fear response to being in a helpless situation as a child. The demonic realm told her that God couldn't keep her safe, but anger and rage could give her power. Elizabeth believed the lies about God and made a demonic alliance by choosing anger and rage. But in truth, anger and rage gave the demonic realm authority to hold her in captivity. While the demonic offer sounded good at the time, dark alliances never work in our favor. Demons do only three things: steal, kill and destroy. (See John 10:10)

Elizabeth's demonic partnership produced rotten fruit (anger, rage, fear, stress) that stole her peace and did nothing to keep her safe. Furthermore, inviting the demonic to set up camp on her land blocked the Holy Spirit from healing her heart. God and the enemy cannot inhabit the same space.

We live in a war zone. Bad stuff happens. But every time it does, we have an open invitation to trust God or partner with the enemy's lies. One leads to light and rest, the other only to darkness. God honors our will. We choose who occupies our land. Land devoted to God experiences the reign of His Peace. Every part of us is either devoted to darkness or devoted to light.

Remember, repentance is an encounter with Truth that heals and reconnects us with the Father.

Until Elizabeth repented of her unholy alliance, that land was legally bound under the enemy's control. Because Elizabeth looked to anger and rage to keep her safe, she missed out on seeing God protect her. This is a common reaction for a child who feels helpless or powerless. However, even these childhood agreements, made in ignorance and fear, give place for the enemy to have a hold on us.

As Elizabeth repented of her unholy agreements and asked God for His protection, she found freedom from fear and anger. The nightmares, buried anger and rage were exchanged for peace and rest. Elizabeth's heart experienced a greater level of God's love for her.

And she slept better.

Emotional Dashboard

When my husband and I were first married, I was clueless about my emotions. Dwight could tell when I was bothered or restless, but his questions annoyed me.

"What are you thinking?" he'd ask.

"I told you already. I'm planning what to make for supper."

"You don't seem yourself," he'd say.

"What are you trying to get at? I'm fine."

"No, you're not. You seem angry."

"I am now! Why do you keep pushing me?"

Growing up, my family was not a safe place to have emotions, let alone talk about them. After being mocked, shamed, ignored, or told, "You want to cry? I'll give you something to cry about!" or "Toughen up!" I learned to shut up and shut down.

After twenty years of stuffed emotions, I no longer knew *how* to feel, let alone *what* I felt. My marriage was a safe place, but I didn't know how to be real anymore. I had been so busy hiding my emotions that I didn't know who I was. It took time for my heart to come back to life and feel what was going on.

The most helpful tool I found to untangle the confusing jumble of thoughts and feelings was an emotive word list. Suddenly all became clear, as I could see a word and immediately identify emotions to communicate them. (See Appendix C at the end of the book.)

Secondly, Dwight persisted in asking me what I was thinking, and how I was doing. While at first this was annoying, because I struggled to know myself and I feared being known. Agreements with rejection will do that. But his persistence forced me to process my thoughts and notice my heart. His words and actions valued me, and so I began to value myself.

Dwight called me up and called me deeper into finding my heart and I am forever grateful. The quality of life and depth of relationships compared with the old and sometimes-comfortable dysfunction has been so worth the work!

My husband likens our emotions to the dashboard of a vehicle. When I'm driving and a dash light comes on, it won't do me any good to ignore it or turn up the radio. When I don't understand the problem (that's every time for me) I take my car to a mechanic who has the right equipment to read the codes and bring an effective solution. Holy Spirit is our code reader.

Hebrews 4:12 says, "For the Word of God is living and active and full of power [making it operative, energizing, and effective]. It is sharper than any two-edged sword, penetrating as far as the division of the soul and spirit [the completeness of a person], and of both joints and marrow [the deepest parts of our nature]; exposing and judging the very thoughts and intentions of the heart."

God's Word (empowered by Holy Spirit) is able to pierce and divide joints (soul) and marrow (spirit). Even though our spirit is intertwined with our soul, God's word cuts past hardened flesh (mind, thoughts, emotions, will and desires) and speaks to our spirit, (the soft place) revealing hidden truth. Holy Spirit tenderly bypasses our walls of protection and pretense with kindness deep in the heart where His Truth can set us free.

When we're really free we don't have to recite verses rapid-fire like, "Do not worry" — as if telling myself "Stop it!" will actually resolve my fear. In this case, the truth my heart needs is that God sees my heart and He cares about my needs. Once I break agreements with the enemy that God is uncaring or ambivalent toward me, then I can feel the happy rest of settling into Truth.

How then will we know we're breaking free?

Quite simply: We start to feel better.

David said it in Psalm 131, vs. 2, "Surely I have calmed and quieted my soul; like a weaned child [resting] with his mother, my soul is like a weaned child within me [composed and freed from discontent]."

Conversely, if we ignore the dash lights, the problem gets worse.

Dwight sat beside me at the kitchen island eating lunch. No, he wasn't eating, he was shoveling lunch down his throat like a fireman on a steam locomotive.

"Dwight, you're eating like it's a race. Why are you so stressed?"

"I'm not stressed. I'm just eating."

"You must be used to it, because I can feel the pressure like we're late for something."

"Well, I can ask God about it..." he ventured.

Later in the day he came back around to the conversation. "So, I asked God about that. And I was stressed. I guess I'm just so used to feeling that pressure to hurry through lunch because there's work that needs to be done. I hadn't realized that I've been operating with the belief that I have to make my own blessing. I guess it's the ugly underbelly of being hyper-responsible."

He continued, "It's so refreshing to center into the truth that God is the author of my blessing. He is with me in all aspects of our business and waiting for me to ask for wisdom and solutions. I forget sometimes that I'm not alone in my workshop. I have so much more fun at work when I'm free to feel His company."

Sometimes we become so used to our own stress that we don't recognize it until others call it out. What a relief to come back to center. God gently picks up the missing truth and hands it back to us. Impatience, frustration, or feeling overwhelmed by our surroundings often signals a need to recalibrate the heart. Don't ignore these symptoms. Find time alone and in the quiet to ask Holy Spirit, "Is there a lie I'm believing, and what truth do I need?"

Remember, when we believe lies about God we make agreements with the enemy. The inevitable result is sin. In Proverbs 4, verse 23, King Solomon says to guard our heart because "from it flow the springs of life."

If you want to know what you truly believe, pay attention to your unfiltered emotional responses. Our minds have knowledge of the truth, but our emotions tell us what we *actually* believe. Belief systems are the seeds of behavior. That is why the devil uses trauma and hardship to sway our belief in the goodness of God.

Emotions expose the belief systems buried in our heart—lies we embraced about God, life, and ourselves disconnect us from our Father. Just as fevers and swollen glands indicate hidden germs, negative emotions expose wrong beliefs about the character of God. Knowlege and belief are not the same. Remember, the enemy can only harass you in the place where you believe his lies.

For example, I may *know* that God is with me, but I *feel* abandoned in a situation. In this case, I really *believe* God has left me alone. Emotions don't follow my head. Emotions always mirror the reality of my heart. And behavior follows emotions. That's why it's so important to pay attention to our emotions. Without them, we'll continue to suffer from a head-knowledge of God that denies heart involvement. We miss the depth of relationship with Him that transforms our inner-man. So too, a head-knowledge of Scripture without the Holy Spirit applying it to my heart is empty.

Early Warning System

"The way of the wicked is like [deep] darkness; they do not know over what they stumble. But the path of the just (righteous) is like the light of dawn, That shines brighter and brighter until [it reaches its full strength and glory in] the perfect day." (Proverbs 4:19, then 18)

Several years ago, my family stumbled into a dangerous situation. Dwight recalls what happened.

That evening the weather had turned cold, and I fired up the coal stove. Our family of six had gathered around to enjoy the heat before we headed for bed. Doe and I were fighting minor headaches. We turned in early hoping to fend off the flu.

Four hours later a pounding headache dragged me out of a deep sleep. Doe woke up and complained of the same. On a hunch, I went downstairs and turned on the computer to research carbon monoxide poisoning.

We didn't have a detector.

Everything I read suggested that drafty, old houses didn't fit the profile for carbon monoxide issues. I decided it must be the flu.

At five a.m. I returned to bed, hoping to push the headache back where it came from.

Less than an hour later, Isaiah (age six), ran to the bathroom feeling sick. Doe got up to check on him. On her way back to bed, she passed out. By the time I got to her she had stopped breathing. I hollered for the older kids and started giving mouth-to-mouth.

Whitney (age ten) and Emily (twelve) showed up. Andrew (eight) slept through everything. I instructed Whitney to get the cell phone and Emily to use the landline downstairs to call friends. Doe started breathing again. I dialed 911.

"Hello, 911, do you need the police, ambulance or fire company?"

"My wife passed out and stopped breathing." I tried to keep my voice steady.

"What is your address, sir?"

I rattled off the wrong address. Thankfully, our local firehouse sits only four blocks down the street. Within minutes the operator, still on the line, asked me to repeat my address. No one was home at the address I had given.

Stress does crazy things, right?! I gave the operator the correct address and noted some concern in her voice.

"Daddy!" Emily's voice sounded odd.

I ran downstairs to find her dazed and sitting on the kitchen floor, leaning against the cabinets with the phone in her limp hand. I pulled her up and hauled her outside.

Two people down. I started to get a clue and updated the operator.

My memory gets blurry after that. Somehow everyone got down the stairs and onto the front porch.

An ambulance came.

Then another.

And a third.

Fire trucks.

We made quite a scene in our small town.

The EMT's loaded Doe into the first ambulance. Emily and Isaiah rode in the second. They hustled Whitney, Andrew and me into the third.

The ambulance carrying Doe turned on the siren and sped away. Apparently, she had been unable to provide lucid answers to simple questions.

After arriving at the ER, nurses double-checked our vitals and administered oxygen for a few hours to cleanse the carbon monoxide from our systems. Six family members. Six hospital beds.

Several hours later, we were discharged to rest and recuperate. Our brains needed to heal from fogginess, our bodies from weakness.

A few days later I spoke with a fireman who had arrived on the scene. He told me their carbon monoxide detectors maxed out as soon as they walked into the house. "At those levels," he said, "a person has less than three minutes to live."

By God's grace, our lives were spared.

Before the ambulances arrived, we literally stumbled around the house with no idea our lives were in danger. Once we diagnosed the problem, we had to make changes for our safety. We aired out the house, breathed concentrated oxygen to replace the poisonous gas, took time to rest and let our brains heal. Most importantly, we installed a carbon monoxide detector to provide an early warning system.

Paying attention to our emotional dashboard is critical. "Watch over your heart with all diligence, for from it flow the springs of life." (Proverbs 4:23)

Negative emotions are the early warning system for our heart. We can't afford to ignore them. If we are to watch over our heart with all diligence, then we must face the negative emotions. The natural human reaction is to avoid, stuff or hide from them, but that can be fatal.

Emotional turmoil indicates a problem.

Conversely, wallowing in negative emotions is equally damaging. All too often, we justify our rights to remain in anger or self-pity. No more. To successfully journey, we must acknowledge our feelings, and allow the Holy Spirit to lead us out of pain and into healing.

"Father, I repent for running from uncomfortable emotions (or wallowing in them). I refuse to run or wallow anymore. I repent of any anger and self-pity. I ask for Your help and courage to allow myself to feel the pain and let You have it. I choose to surrender my pain, trauma, anger and self-pity to You. Please come and heal my heart."

Roots and Fruits

As previously noted, positive emotions are the result of a heart rooted in the truth about God's love. Conversely, most negative emotions* indicate underlying wrong beliefs. Any area (body, mind, thoughts, emotions, will, desires, relationships) where we don't experience inner-peace can be restored to truth.

Good fruit comes from truth, bad fruit comes from lies.

Stress, impatience, worry, fear, anxiety, jealousy, anger, rage, restlessness, dread, control, manipulation and greed are all bad fruit. (Gal. 5:19-21)

Good fruit evidences itself as peace, love, joy, patience, kindness, goodness, gentleness, self control, and faithfulness. (Gal. 5:22-23)

In our journey, Dwight and I often found ourselves saying, "But this [negative emotion] is normal. Most people feel this way. Can I really expect to live without it?"

In Matthew 6, when Jesus said, "don't worry about your life," he was highlighting a negative emotion that was part of his audience's "normal" experience. After all, most of his audience lived hand-to-mouth or dependent on seasonal rains. He didn't just say, don't worry. He showed them *how* to stop worrying. Jesus connected the command with the truth that our Father cares and provides for us. Reciting the verse, "Do not worry" over and over can't bring us into peace. However, rejecting the lie that we are alone and fully embracing the truth of our Father's active love and care will bring us back to rest.

When we settle for what's "normal" for the general population, we miss what God intended.

God did not create us to survive in an earth-bound experience of "normal." The kingdom of heaven excels beyond any earthly kingdom. God made us to thrive — to live an abundant life. We were designed to experience joy, peace, and love as our new normal. We are not victims to our circumstances, the world or emotions. Christ empowered us to live above "normal".

Emotions expose what's going on "under the hood." Don't be afraid of negative emotions but use them as a tool to see what is going on in your heart. It may take investigation, but its too important to ignore. Escape, masking and pretend actually harden the heart. (Deuteronomy 3:8)

Hardening the heart didn't work out well for Pharoah or the Israelites in the wilderness. As Isaiah said, "For this nation's heart has grown hard, and with their ears they hardly hear, and they have [tightly] closed their eyes, otherwise they would see with their eyes, and hear with their ears, and understand with their heart, and turn [to Me] and I would heal them [spiritually]." (Matthew 13:15)

We cannot live numb and be alive. **We must feel to heal**. Facing buried pain and the lies attached to it can feel overwhelming. Take courage, Holy Spirit leads with kindness and gentleness. Our broken hearts need to be loved back to life through the experience of our Father's love and care. Allowing Him to comfort and heal the pain brings truth (through experiencing relationship with Him) to the deepest parts of the heart.

Here's a simple way to get started. Before we identify underlying beliefs, we must first learn how to tune-in to our emotions. Read through the list of emotions at the end of this book **(Appendix C, Emotive Word Lists)** and pick 3 positive emotions and 3 negative emotions that you identify with. Fill in the blanks...

"I feel (name the emotion) when (name the situation)."

If identifying emotions is a struggle, practice this exercise every day. Emotional awareness is the first step toward self-discovery and healing.

Luke 6:45, says, "The [intrinsically] good man produces what is good and honorable and moral out of the good treasure [stored] in his heart; and the [intrinsically] evil man produces what is wicked and depraved out of the evil [in his heart]; for his mouth speaks from the overflow of his heart."

* Disclaimer: Negative emotions that stem from grief and loss, such as a death or betrayal, (or jealousy in the case of betrayal) cannot be simply taken to the cross to be rid of. Death (loss) requires time to mourn (release the person) and betrayal wounds the spirit. As wounds on the body need time and attention for healing, it is the same with our spirit. Let out those feelings and bring them to God, our Comforter.

Flashing Lights

What do you do when your brain won't stop chasing it's tail? The emotional turmoil and mental bombardment allow no rest.

The following framework provides a starting point to address the flashing lights and to understand what's driving the turmoil.

Simply put, here's how to feel better!

This process can be used on your own, but it is often more beneficial to take this journey with a friend. Our own core beliefs can be so familiar that we fail to see issues clearly. Having a friend bring a more objective perspective is like putting on a pair of glasses for the first time.

This is not an intellectual or mental quest. Quiet your thoughts. Invite the Holy Spirit (who resides in your spirit) to lead you. "Now the mind of the flesh is death [both now and forever — because it pursues sin]; but the mind of the

Spirit is life and peace [the spiritual well-being that comes from walking with God — both now and forever]" (Romans 8:6).

Ask Holy Spirit for revelation and guidance through these four steps.

#1 Identify the Emotion

Figure out exactly what you're feeling. Use the process outlined in the last chapter. This may feel like trying on pairs of shoes until one fits right. Go through the emotive word list (at the end of the book) until you are able to identify the exact emotion. Write it down.

#2 Find Hurt and Forgive

When and where did this emotion start? Was there a situation that caused me pain or turmoil?

Because lies about God usually collect around pain and trauma, identifying the hurt and forgiving those involved helps to clear the air and zero in.

An emotional response may be triggered by current circumstances, but more often a strong emotional reaction indicates an unresolved past wound of a similar nature. Ask Holy Spirit to reveal the source; the original cause of pain. When the original wound is healed, you will stop reacting to current situations in an unhealthy manner. In order to break the chains to pain, we first need to both find the place of hurt and forgive everyone involved. We will take a closer look at trauma in a later chapter.

Be aware that perceived hurts still cause pain. Perceived hurts, as well as intentional hurts, function as a doorway for the enemy's lies. Someone does not have to intentionally hurt you to cause you pain.

Pay attention to the Holy Spirit's leading. Ask Him to reveal anyone you need to forgive. Name who you are forgiving, how they hurt you, and your own sin. Be specific. Make it personal.

God, You know the hurt I carry. I choose to forgive __(name the individual)__ and lay down my offense. I lay down any and all anger, grudges, rage, bitterness, revenge that I have carried. I release this person to You and trust in Your justice. Help me to continue to forgive and not rehearse the wrongs. Keep me focused on You. I repent for __(my own sin)__ .

#3 Expose Lies and Repent

What did I believe about God, myself or others because of that situation?

Lies make us feel bad and drive poor behavior. If we want to live in victory, we have to identify the ways we have agreed with the enemy's twisted view of God, ourselves and others. The enemy causes pain, trauma and offense to make us more susceptible to his lies. When we experience wounding, the enemy lies to us about ourselves, others and the goodness of God. Lies slander God's character and break down the foundation of our relationship with Him. We don't want to be close to someone we don't trust.

Because the enemy is a liar (there is no truth in him), any way we agree with what he says is an agreement with a lie. (John 8:44) And when we agree with a lie, we give the enemy a piece of our heart. His lies then have the right to influence our emotions, will, desires, thoughts and relationships. When we buy into the enemy's lies, we share in his misery.

Repentance is a legal process by which we break contract with the devil.

Ask Holy Spirit to reveal specifically what lies the enemy whispered into your pain.

Here are just a few examples of lies:

Lies

- I am alone/ abandoned.
- No one loves me.
- I'm rejected, unwanted.
- I am forgotten.
- I am a failure.
- My sin is too great.
- Life is too hard.
- I don't need anyone. I am better off alone.
- I don't have enough./ I am poor.
- I must take care of myself.

Once Holy Spirit has shown you what lies you've believed, repent for them, renounce them from your life (declare you want nothing more to do with them). Make the prayer personal; be specific.

"Father, I repent for believing the lie that _____ . I repent for all the ways I have partnered with that lie by   (name the sin) . "

Ask Holy Spirit to gather up all the dirt, hurt and broken relationships that have resulted from the lie. Take that pile to the cross where Christ forgives your sin and gives you beauty for ashes.

"But we have renounced the disgraceful things hidden because of shame; not walking in trickery or adulterating the word of God, but by stating the truth [openly and plainly], we commend ourselves to everyone's conscience in the sight of God," (2 Cor. 4:2).

#4 Receive Truth

Once you have repented of agreeing with the lie that drives this negative emotion or sin pattern, ask Holy Spirit to lead you into all truth. (John 16:13) Pay attention; the Holy Spirit speaks in many ways. He may give you a picture, a scripture, a feeling, or a memory that reveals what is true, what He thinks or how He feels about you. Boil the truth down to a simple sentence or picture, write it down and rehearse it aloud and often.

Here are examples of truths found in Scripture:

Truths

- I am never alone or abandoned. Dt. 31:6,

- God is good, He is attentive to me. Jn. 10:10, Ps. 34:4-8, 5,17

- I am chosen; He delights in me. Ps. 139, Eph. 1:11-14

- I have always been loved. Jer. 31:3; Zeph. 3:17

- God never forgets me. I am always on His mind. Is. 49:14-16

- I am victorious. Rm. 8:37; Eph. 3:20

- Christ is my righteousness. Eph. 2:8-9; Ps. 103:1-12

- God is my strength. Is. 41:10; Phil. 4:6-9

- He gives me all I need. Ps. 16:2; Pt. 1:3; Phil. 4:13

- God made me for relationship with Him and others. Jn. 15:4-6; 17:21-23

- God is my Provider. I have all I need. Ps. 34:8-10; Mt. 6:25-34

- He takes good care of me. 1 Pt. 5:7; Jer. 29:11; Zech. 4:6

You can use the following prayer as a guide.

"Father, I receive the truth about You that _____. Holy Spirit come and fill me with Your Truth. Thank you for Your forgiveness and healing, in Jesus' name!"

You'll know you're making progress when you feel God's Peace. If you don't feel better, there are probably more lies at work. Go back to step one and repeat the process.

This exchange of truth for lies is a lifestyle.

Interact with God throughout your day. As you are attentive to Him, He will continue to speak to you about who He is and how much He loves you. If the Holy Spirit doesn't answer you immediately, be patient. There have been times that the answer came hours or days later. Keep the eyes and ears of your heart open to Him. He tends to show up when and how we least expect it!

"...what man is there among you who, if his son asks for bread, will [instead] give him a stone? Or if he asks for a fish, will [instead] give him a snake? If you then, evil (sinful by nature) as you are, know how to give good and advantageous gifts to your children, how much more will your Father who is in heaven [perfect as He is] give what is good and advantageous to those who keep on asking Him." (Matthew 7:9-11)

Journal this process with Holy Spirit. A record of your inner journey provides an invaluable reminder of what God showed you and you'll need the truth again in the following days to stand your ground. Look up Scriptures to go with them. Memorize them. Keep them on index cards in your Bible, on your refrigerator, on the mirror, by your bed, in your car. Soak; meditate; fill your mind with the truth that replaces the old thought patterns and beliefs.

The enemy often uses forgetfulness and confusion to keep you in his lies. After all, this is a war for your soul. When you start feeling the same negative emotion again, go back and rehearse the truth that brought you rest.

Forgiveness

We had an uninvited guest in our mudroom. With a wood stove, dog food, four walls and a roof, the room offered significant comfort and provisions for a mouse in winter.

We set a sticky trap. But C.L.B. (Cheeky Little Blighter) dusted the top with sawdust, then walked across and took the cheese. Several attempts produced the same result.

Eventually we went old-school and purchased the original mouse trap. The spring-loaded, snap-your-thumb-if-you're-not-careful sort of trap. We baited it with peanut butter and pulled back the kill bar against the spring's tension, secured the trigger and waited.

Still the mouse outsmarted us. In the morning, we found the trap had been sprung with a wood splinter and someone had gobbled up the peanut butter. It couldn't have been our dog.

We decided that if C.L.B. was that smart, he could stay.

The Greek word for the trigger on a trap is 'skándalon.' It appears 25 times in the New Testament. According to the Strong's Lexicon of the Greek, 'skándalon' is the same word used by Jesus and New Testament writers for our English word 'offense'.

If you want to catch a monkey, every villager knows that chasing him is a waste of time and energy. It is far easier to bore a hole in a hollowed-out coconut just big enough for a monkey to get his paw into. Then, place a piece of fruit inside the coconut and fasten it to a tree. A monkey, being greedy by nature, will reach in, but the hole is too small to extract his fist full of fruit.

Since the monkey is unwilling to let go of the beloved fruit, the villager comes along and easily bags him. At the price of his freedom, the monkey will refuse to open his fist. **The monkey makes his own bondage.**

Every time we refuse to forgive, we take the enemy's bait. Offense equals entrapment. It's so easy that Satan has prisons full of offended people. The Amplified Bible refers to these people as "overly sensitive and easily angered" (1 Corinthians 13:4-5).

While trust does have to be earned, to follow the way of love means we do not hold onto offense. To forget how we've been wronged (as though the event never happened) is not realistic or even safe in some cases. But we do need to forget in the sense of not rehearsing the sin, the pain or the offense.

At times we even need to forgive God. No, God never does wrong. But often we harbor bitterness and judgments against Him because He didn't do things our way. We need to repent for thinking we know better than Him. He is God, therefore He is Judge. Take yourself off the throne; agree that He knows best. Trust that His Goodness is better than we understand.

Forgiveness isn't an easy choice, but it is an act of the will. It does not depend on feelings. Open your mouth and say, "I choose to forgive so-and-so." Your words are powerful. Use your mouth and your will to lead you into the decision to forgive. When you speak, the spirit realm is activated. **Forgiveness is also a legal process by which we break our self-inflicted bondage to pain.**

Ask God for help. He always gives the strength to do what He asks. I know there can be significant, life-altering offenses that require great levels of trust to give to God. But we cannot heal or be forgiven ourselves, without forgiving others.

Matthew 6:14-15 tells us, "For if you forgive others their trespasses [their reckless and willful sins], your heavenly Father will also forgive you. **But if you do not forgive others [nurturing your hurt and anger with the result that it interferes with your relationship with God], then your Father will not forgive your trespasses**." (Emphasis mine)

Common Lies about Forgiveness:

- To forgive means it didn't hurt, or that I don't matter.
- If I forgive, there will be no justice.
- Forgiveness lets the offender off the hook.
- If I forgive, it will happen again. I'll become a doormat.
- I have to hold unforgiveness to balance the scales of

justice.

- I can't forgive while I still feel hurt and anger.

- By holding onto anger, hatred, bitterness, revenge, I will ensure justice.

- In order to forgive, I have to forget.

The Truth:

- By holding onto unforgiveness, we get in the way of God's justice. (Prov. 24:17-18)

- Forgiveness frees us from pain and bondage to the offender. (Mt. 18:21-35)

- Unforgiveness causes emotional, mental and physical harm to us, not the one who hurt us. (Prov. 14:14, 21-22; Ps. 32:1-6)

- Forgiveness is a gift; no one deserves it. We all need it. (Ps. 130:1-4)

- God forgave us a bigger debt. We hurt Him more than anyone hurt us. We forgive because God forgave us. (Ps. 130:1-4; Is. 53:3-6,10-12)

- Forgiveness isn't a feeling. It's a choice of the will. (Dt. 30:15-20)

- It doesn't mean it didn't hurt or that you don't matter.

- **Forgiveness and trust are not the same.** Trust must be earned. Forgiveness is a gift.

- A person's position NEVER entitles them to your

trust.* (ie: parent, child, pastor, politician) (Prov. 29:5; James 3:1; Mt. 23:8-12)

- Forgiveness does not mean I take down protective boundaries. God set boundaries, we need them too. (Jer. 5:21-25)

- A person's behavior ALWAYS determines the boundaries you must set. (See the book of Proverbs regarding boundaries and relationships)

- Forgiveness means I stop rehearsing the pain and focus on Christ instead. (Phil 3:13-14,: 4:8)

- Forgiveness is a choice to trust God's perfect justice. (Is. 211-12; Ps. 37:5-8)

- Forgiveness may not forget but chooses not to remember, recall or rehearse. (Prov. 17:9)

*It is important to understand that forgiveness and trust are two separate issues. **Just because I forgive someone, does NOT mean they are trustworthy!** Forgiveness is a gift that you give, because Christ forgave you. No one earns forgiveness. It's a gift that cost God everything! Trust, however, is earned. A person must prove themselves trustworthy through time-tested change of behavior.

Forgive, Repent, Receive

The daily journey of exchanging Truth for lies is how we walk in the Spirit. It's how we disciple ourselves into a Kingdom mindset. It is a daily conversation with God and a bridge we use to lead others back to a place of rest. Where possible, we process our journey with others who can offer objectivity where we are blinded by familiar hurts and agreements.

Brittney (not her real name) came over to pray with us because of significant inner turmoil. Only the important parts of our dialogue are included. The stories and emotions have been summarized and the comfortable, conversational padding has been removed. Consequently, it may sound clinical, but it will help to illustrate the process.

#1 Identify the Emotion

"What's going on, Brittney?" I asked.

"Thanks for letting me stop by," she said. "It's been a really tough week. I've been battling thoughts of hatred toward myself. I'm constantly down on myself. I know it's wrong. I try to stop. I keep telling myself that God loves and accepts me, but the thoughts are relentless."

#2 Find hurt and Forgive

"When did the negative self-talk start?" I asked, "Did something happen to trigger this, or has this always been there?"

"It has been going on for a long time," she said, "I'm not sure when it began, but it has been worse recently."

"Okay, let's ask God when this started," I suggested. "Pay attention to any pictures or memories He might bring to mind. Don't edit what He gives you. It may seem insignificant at first, but it could be important."

"God," Brittney said, "You know I feel like I'm going out of my mind! Would You please show me when this negative self-talk began?"

Brittney listened quietly for a few minutes, allowing the Holy Spirit to lead. "A few memories came to mind," she said, "I must have been six when a friend made fun of my singing. I had another memory from when I was about eleven. My best friend left me to join the group of popular kids.

"That's hard. I'm sorry that happened to you," I said. "Are you willing to forgive those kids, so you're no longer tied to that pain?"

"Yes." Brittney sighed. "I choose to forgive Brandon for laughing at me. I forgive Rachel for abandoning me. And I forgive all the 'popular' kids who stole my friendship with Rachel, even if they didn't intend to hurt me."

#3 Expose Lies and Repent

"So," I said, "let's ask Holy Spirit to reveal what lies you believed."

Brittney prayed quietly, then said, "I guess I believe God made me inferior, stupid, and ugly." Brittney grimaced when she said it aloud. "I think I've tried to hide and become what I thought others wanted. They might like who I pretend to be, but I'm always afraid of rejection. I never really found out if the real me is lovable, because nobody knows the real me."

"So, do you want to get rid of those lies?"

"Yes! I'm embarrassed just hearing them out loud. Would you mind leading me through that. I'm having a hard time focusing."

"Sure. You can repeat after me: Father, I repent for believing you made me inferior, stupid or ugly. I repent for making an idol out of people's opinion. I've allowed their acceptance to matter more than Yours. I break off the lies that I'm not good enough, or that something is wrong with how You made me. I choose to stop looking to people for approval. I will no longer give them the right to determine my value or decide if I'm lovable. I don't want to live in fear of rejection anymore!

"I repent for jealousy and comparing myself to others. I repent for judging people in the same way I felt judged. I choose to seek Your approval rather than man's approval."

#4 Receive Truth

I let Brittney sit with that for a minute, then asked, "Now, what does God say about who you are? Let's ask God to tell you what He thinks about you."

"Okay." Brittney continued, "Father God, show me what You think of me."

Brittney sat and listened for a while with her eyes closed. Then she said, "I got a picture of Him singing a duet with me." She smiled. "He made me to love music because He loves it too. He made me to sing with Him. That picture of Him singing with me takes away all the hurt about others not accepting me. When I feel Him enjoying my music, I don't care what other people think anymore!"

"I love that!" I responded. "God takes great delight in who you are and in being with you. He didn't make you inferior to anyone. Popularity is the world's way of measuring a person's value, and it doesn't see the heart. God knows our heart and He loves who He made us to be. Why don't you declare that out loud?"

"Father," said said, "You call me chosen, accepted, loved, and beautiful. I receive this truth in my heart, in Jesus' name. Help me to keep that picture in my heart of You and me singing together. Help me to guard my mind and emotions from the lies that I don't measure up."

"How are you feeling now?" I asked.

Brittney took a deep breath. "I feel so much better. My mind is quieter already."

Here's an example of what this conversation might look like when we're alone. (Not a true story.)

Blue light illuminated the nightstand as I poked my phone. Three o'clock. Too early to get up. I flopped back on the pillow, trying to find a comfortable spot. The problem wasn't the pillow. An internal alarm was ringing. It took a while for me to come to my senses.

I felt awful. My internal search engine worked overtime to find something I did wrong.

Eventually, it landed. I'd missed an appointment. I even had it on my calendar!

I sighed, sick with guilt.

#1 Identify the Emotion

What exactly do I feel? I asked myself and the Holy Spirit.

Shame. I feel shame.

I should feel shame, right?

Wrong. Shame is not a pathway to righteousness. Shame is not my inheritance. I know Christ took shame and punishment for me. I know my inheritance in Christ is righteousness, peace, and joy.

But the shame stuck like bird droppings on a windshield.

#2 Find hurt and Forgive

When did I first feel this way?

I thought for a while, and asked God to lead the way. I closed my eyes and gave myself permission to be vulnerable.

A flash of memory. I wasn't sure exactly how old I was, but I'd tried to help dad unload a bag of grass seed from the car. I wanted to be strong for him. I wanted him to be proud. The heavy bag snagged on the sharp bumper and tore wide open. Seeds poured out like water. Dad was livid. "What do you think you are you doing? Look at this mess!"

That was when I first felt shame like this.

I chose to forgive myself for spilling the grass seed. I forgave myself for failing. I forgave Dad for his anger.

Then I forgave myself for missing the appointment.

#3 Expose Lies and Repent

Holy Spirit, what lies did I agree to way back then?

It took a few minutes to find words for it all. I blamed myself for Dad's anger. After all, I thought he had a right to be angry with me. I believed I was a failure. I wasn't strong enough. I wasn't capable. I agreed with shame. In the end, I believed I had to "get things right" in order to be valued.

I could feel the Peace of God at the door of my heart. Just

putting words on all those lies pushed the accusations back.

One by one, I repented for agreeing with the lies that were harassing me. I repented for agreeing with the lie that I am a failure, that I am not strong enough, that I have to get it right to be loved.

#4 Receive Truth

I took a deep breath, and listened as the Holy Spirit showed me truth.

I'm allowed to be human.

I don't have to perform to be loved.

God made me capable.

God is proud of me.

He's not offended by my weakness.

My value is set by God, not others.

What others think of me doesn't change my worth.

I could feel the Peace of God fill my heart. The search engine blinked off. I felt better. Even the pillow felt better.

Sentry Duty

After walking through repentance and cleaning house with God, we need to be on the alert to the enemy's subtle tactics to take back what he once had. Keep the truth in front of you. Ask Holy Spirit for His help and protection.

We live in a small town — we don't even have a mailman. So we go to the post office to get our mail. Each day I sort the bills, paperwork and cards from incoming junk. Occasionally, I open the envelopes to categorize them.

Some look important, even urgent, like the envelopes stamped, 'time-sensitive material.' One time I was even a specially selected winner! Those look almost authentic. Almost. The fine print revealed an urgent deadline for me to get another credit card or insurance policy or get-rich-quick plan.

As if that weren't enough, I get email, too. Every day I delete or unsubscribe from unwanted rubbish. Some emails need to be checked for validity and importance. Others shouldn't even be opened. Finally, I'm left with what I need or want to read.

Then I flag the important ones.

Discipling our heart requires we sort through the daily barrage of thoughts and information. In Proverbs 4:20-27, King Solomon says that the key to life—to health in one's whole body— is to watch over the heart. Even history illustrates why it is imperative to take every thought captive.

Communists used a constant stream of false information to capture an entire society without war. Over multiple generations, their propaganda worked its way into the mainstream. Some believed whatever authorities told them while others' resistance gradually eroded under the continual barrage. Persistent indoctrination shifted a national paradigm until once-obvious lies became culturally acceptable.

This is exactly how Satan operates. He floods our emotions with subtle impressions, a steady harassment of ideas, temptations or thoughts. If he gets us to agree with his message, or give up fighting against them, he wins.

What we don't forbid, we allow. Passivity is implicit agreement. I can agree with God and empower truth in my life, or I can agree with lies and empower the enemy. Remember, agreements confer governmental authority over our lives.

Paul urges us in 2 Corinthians 10:4-5, "The weapons of our warfare are not physical [weapons of flesh and blood]. Our weapons are divinely powerful for the destruction of fortresses. We are destroying sophisticated arguments and every exalted and proud thing that sets itself up against the [true] knowledge of God, and we are taking every thought and purpose captive to the obedience of Christ".

Ancient and medieval cities were built with walls surrounding them for protection against invaders. At certain points along the wall, a watchman or sentry would be tasked with keeping an eye on all approaches to the city. Both King Solomon and Peter admonish us to set a watchman over our hearts to guard the entrances to our lives: people, relationships, technology, music, literature, news.

God gave us the Holy Spirit to warn and protect us. If we don't listen to Him, we are in danger of invasion. The Holy Spirit not only alerts us, He reveals the truth anytime we ask. In times of confusion or doubt, ("something doesn't feel/sound right") ask for His wisdom.

Troubleshooting

Common roadblocks in our connection to Father

Disappointments

One Sunday we entered a sanctuary filled with the sounds of worship. Normally, this is a vulnerable place where I easily feel God's presence. But today I felt heavy, as though my body didn't want to engage. All around me, others were focused, arms raised, singing their hearts out. My heart just wasn't in it.

Rather than force it, I sat down to pray privately. "God what is going on? Why does it feel so hard to worship today? Is there some way that I'm holding offense against You?"

As soon as I asked the question, disappointment rolled over me as images came to mind of things that hadn't worked out in the past months. Finances, failed appliances, relationships, health issues, tough week with our business. It might not have been a big deal if it hadn't been for several years of similar disappointments one on top of the other. When would it end?

"Really, God, that too? Haven't we been through enough already?"

Once again, I gave that week's disappointment, and the last month, and the past 3 months, the past year to God and let Him have it. ALL of it. Again. I forgave Him for not cooperating with MY plan, MY timeline. I repented and renounced the lie that He did me wrong.

Then I chose to believe that God's heart toward me is good. He has good stored up for me. (Jer. 29:11) I received the good things that happened that I didn't really want to see because they didn't fit the box of complaints that I was stockpiling. I thanked Him for the many gifts He gave us. A full pantry, warm house, soft beds, bills paid (even if it was close), a loving family...

"Okay, God, You can have my disappointment and my box of complaints. I'll take the good You have for me instead."

I felt Him grieve the pain with me and peace filled my soul again. Worship was sweeter than it had been in a long time.

The ability to hear from the Holy Spirit is imperative to our healing journey. Interacting with the Holy Spirit is, after all, the primary benefit of our salvation and, according to Jesus, even better than walking side by side with the incarnate Christ. If you struggle to hear from the Holy Spirit – don't beat yourself up! We've all been there.

We are all affected by the wear and tear of life. If we don't tend the garden of our heart, the weeds of disappointment, frustration, grief and loss will choke out our love. The Father feels distant, silent, uncaring, unreachable.

DISAPPOINTMENTS

We are a priesthood of believers. The job of the Old Testament priest was first and foremost to minister **to God**. Not to people. To God.

No matter what the weather, the priests kept the fire alive on the altar. It was also the priest's job to keep the lampstand burning in the Temple at all times. The wicks had to be trimmed regularly and special oil prepared ahead of time, so it didn't run out.

In the same way, our worship is a lifestyle of interaction with Father, the continual turning of our affection toward Him. Staying in love requires that my heart remain open, vulnerable and soft toward the things of God. An offended heart closes its ears to His voice. And God feels far away. Complaining, impatience and bitterness indicate that we don't see our Father correctly. Our eyes become blind to His goodness. Hardness of heart and skepticism set in, then unbelief and eventually rebellion. (Heb. 3:8-12)

Life's biggest challenge is keeping our love alive. (Rev. 2:4-5) Trauma, pain, loss, frustration and disappointment can create callouses on our heart. Every moment we have the opportunity to choose connection or disconnection with the Father. Tending our relationship with the Father is our foremost priority. When we keep focus on being in love with Him, all other relationships will receive the flow of health and life that grows out of that Love.

The struggle to be physically or emotionally present in worship is a clue to unresolved pain that's in the way. Fully entering into worship means our whole person is engaged—body, mind, thoughts, emotions will, and desire. It isn't normal to say we love our family and not show affection to them. Any time you feel uncomfortable, agitated, or blocked in worship or prayer, ask Holy Spirit to show you the reason.

If friendship with our Abba, Father has become a duty or feels stale, it's time to clean out old ashes and stoke the fire. A heart is kept sensitive by honesty and vulnerability. Pain and offense must be released in order to experience the Father's compassion. Acknowledge the pain; grieve the loss. In place of trauma, pain and offense we find His comfort waiting for us.

Jesus understands our hardships and pain. "For we do not have a High Priest who is unable to sympathize *and* understand our weaknesses *and* temptations, but One who has been tempted [knowing exactly how it feels to be human] in every respect as *we are, yet* without [committing any] sin. Therefore let us [with privilege] approach the throne of grace [that is, the throne of God's gracious favor] with confidence *and* without fear, so that we may receive mercy [for our failures] and find [His amazing] grace to help in time of need [an appropriate blessing, coming just at the right moment]." (Heb. 4:15-16)

A Question of Character

The Jews held such respect for the Almighty God that they wouldn't even speak His name aloud. But Jesus presented a totally new and unexpected picture of God as a kind and loving Daddy. "Abba" was the first familiar and intimate name a child used for his papa.

Everything Jesus said and did was exactly what the Father would have said and done. (John 5:19)

Jesus described Himself as the Good Shepherd who lays down (sacrifices) His life for the sheep. (Jn. 10:11) How many Kings do you know who died willingly in the place of criminals?!

He also said, "I came that they may have and enjoy life, and have it in abundance (to the full, till it overflows)." (John 10:10b)

Jesus stood in the synagogue and declared, "the Spirit of the Lord God is upon Me, because the Lord has anointed and commissioned Me to bring good news to the humble and afflicted; He has sent me to bind up [the wounds of] the brokenhearted, to proclaim release [from confinement and condemnation] to the [physical and spiritual] captives and freedom to prisoners." (Isaiah 61:1)

Startled and delighted by this earth-shattering revelation of the character of God, people turned out in droves to see Jesus.

Jesus' ministry revealed the Father's heart by demonstrating His authority and willingness to forgive all sin and heal all diseases. (Psalm 103:3) "And great crowds came to Him, bringing with them the lame, crippled, blind, mute, and many others, and they put them down at His feet; and He healed them." (Matthew 15:30)

Jesus came to give us a living picture of the Father. Jesus told us, "Anyone who has seen Me has seen the Father." (John 14:9-10) In essence He was saying, "You don't understand the Father's heart. I have come so you could get the right perspective." Jesus was like a ladder helping us see over the wall of religion into the Father's heart.

They needed it. We need it.

Not once do we read of Jesus giving the 'gift' of sickness or disease to build character and develop maturity. Not once did He take a life. No one who came to Him went away with more problems.

Not ever.

Jesus was "the exact representation and perfect imprint of His

[Father's] essence" (Hebrews 1:3)

God sent His only Son to give us "life abundantly" in exchange for sin and sickness.

To claim God gives sickness, death and disease runs counter to the mission of Jesus and violates the entire gospel message. The "gospel" means *good* news. He paid the ultimate price to liberate us from the curse of sin, why would He give it back?

We need to be very careful not to write theology based on human understanding or experience. Our theology must be based on the Word of God. If our experience doesn't line up, *we* need to change, not rewrite what God says about Himself. We don't have to understand or make sense of all that God says about Himself, we just have to believe it. Relinquish control and knowledge in exchange for trust.

Jesus told us the *devil* (thief) "comes only in order to steal and kill and destroy." (John 10:10). That, according to Scripture, is the devil's job description and character analysis. Satan loves it when we blame God for his work!

Since the Fall, humanity has lived in a war zone. Bad stuff happens and things break. The enemy has always been bent on destruction. He hates that we are made in God's image, therefore he is out to destroy us.

Sin and suffering were never God's plan for us. Suffering entered the world because of man's choices. Though mankind rebelled, God made a way for our redemption at the cost of His own Son. Our Father has always been about life, healing, restoration and abundance. Redemption is God's character and job description.

When we slip into believing that God takes life, withholds what is good, causes evil or gives sickness and disease, that single shift of blame perverts the entire gospel. Worse, it distorts our trust in a kind and loving Father. God embodies goodness. "In Him there is no darkness at all [no sin, so wickedness, no imperfection]" (1 John 1:5).

Perfect love casts out fear. Fear births survivalists who fail to invest in today, who hide from life and who prepare for disaster. The man who fears God hides, hardens himself, or runs. The heart that understands the Father's loving intentions can entrust himself fully to Him. That man can live boldly, understanding that God's purposes for him are entirely good.

A man who doesn't trust that God is good will not feel safe to submit to Him. If you have believed the lie that God is a taker, now is the time to lay that down. Use the following prayer to get you started, but make it specific and personal to your life.

Father, I repent for believing the lie that You take or withhold good. I acknowledge the bad that has happened in my life is a result of a fallen world, the enemy, or the consequences of sin.

I call to mind that the devil is the liar, thief, destroyer and murderer. I renounce the lie that You have hurt me or caused the pain in my life. I repent for all rebellion or anger I have harbored against You.

I will no longer place the blame on You. I lay all these lies and hurts at the cross to be remembered no more. Cleanse my mind and heart of all deception.

I declare the truth that You, God, are light. You are for me and have only good plans for me. In You there is no darkness at all. You came to give me abundant life. (Jeremiah 29:11; Romans 8:28)

Holy Spirit, heal my heart. Show me the truth about my Father. Give me new eyes and a clear mind to stay focused on Your goodness. I want to know You and trust You with my heart.

Divided Heart

Rob had been abusive since the beginning. For years he kept his wife, Sonya, dancing to his demands. (Not their real names.) Rob used anger and manipulation to control his family. They were too afraid of his anger to oppose him, but keeping him happy kept them in bondage. Finally, Sonya and the kids got out.

Their church and community thought Rob was amazing. He was gregarious, happy, funny, generous, served in the church and provided well for his family. What wasn't to like?

Abusive? No way. Not Rob.

Sonya spent years covering it up. She and the kids hid the truth to maintain appearances. After all, Christians aren't supposed to have problems like that.

The opinion of people was an idol the whole family served. They used deceit and pretend to cover for Rob's anger, control, and abuse. They believed love and honor meant they should help to hide Rob's sin. Now, when they finally told the truth, no one believed them.

Sonya's heart was divided between following God and trying to keep people happy. She had to first give up the idolatry of public image (fear of man) in order to have the inner strength to walk away and make healthy boundaries.

Fear, disoriented focus, and unholy exchanges divide our heart and interfere with our connection to Father.

Fear

Fear drives an idolatry often mislabeled "wisdom." **Fear, the opposite of trust in God, should never lead our decision making.** When we operate with a core belief that we're on our own, that we have to take care of ourselves, or that God won't come through for us – we are not walking in faith. Instead, we serve the idol of fear.

It's "easy" to expect God to come through for the missionary in China or the traveling evangelist, but not so easy to trust God with my family, my health, my taxes or my broken dishwasher. Every decision is either made in rest (trust in God) or made in fear (idolatry).

Man's fear, under the guise of "wisdom," says obedience to God needs to make sense. Needs to be 'safe'. When we feel the pull of God to take a step of faith, we can't let man's wisdom disqualify the Holy Spirit's leading because it isn't logical.

Instead of walking in obedience, we analyze risks, study financial models, safety nets and critical redundancies. We believe that we're walking in "godly wisdom" when we have all our ducks in a row and every financial contingency worked out ahead of time. None of these things are bad. However, when they keep us from stepping out in faith, they become an idol. An idol is anything we have to check with before we obey God.

Fear can lead us to take or keep a job that violates the God-spouse-family-work-ministry ladder of priority because we "need" the paycheck, the health package, or retirement plan. After all, "I have to provide for my family."

Of course, God calls us to be good stewards. We are called to provide for our family. However, if our quest to take care of our family causes us to violate God's order of priorities, then we aren't walking in righteousness. After all, God is the source of provision. That's what Matthew chapter six is all about.

Man's "wisdom" has become a cover for our lack of trust in God. Fear lives in caution and suspicion. Pessimism, fear, anxiety and control stem from an orphan heart. Fear deceives us into thinking we are the providers. We believe the lie that God is not good, He isn't powerful enough to come through for us or He doesn't deliver to our address.

The great men of faith recorded in Scripture would have been considered fools in their moment of decision. In some cases, those moments lasted decades. (Think Noah, Abraham, Joseph, David) Too often, man's "wisdom" is a smokescreen for cowardice. This "wisdom" keeps pioneers from breaking into new territory. It blocks innovations and withholds breakthroughs in technology, medicine, engineering and art. Worst of all, it is a barrier to trusting the Father.

Faith rarely looked wise. Faith is "**an inherent trust and enduring confidence in the power, wisdom and goodness of God]... without faith it is impossible to [walk with God and] please Him**, for whoever comes [near] to God must [necessarily] believe that God exists and that **He rewards those who [earnestly and diligently] seek Him.**" (Hebrews 11:2,3,6; boldface, mine)

When God called Abraham to leave his city and family to go into the unknown, I think we miss the context of what that meant. Abraham did more than take a road trip without a destination in mind.

Cities, in those days, were surrounded with walls. The kings provided an army, watchtowers, gates, water and food supply to protect the city. People gathered there for safety. Beyond those walls marauders stalked the weak and lonely to raid and plunder.

City life meant access to markets, food, and wells. There were no rest stops, convenience stores, or camel service centers in the desert. Leaving the city wasn't merely a social loss, but a loss of medical care, law and order, civil infrastructure and business network. Abraham followed God into a vulnerable place where massacre and starvation were real possibilities.

Abrahams' departure was an enormous, illogical, stupid step of obedience. Fear for our safety, fear of the future, fear of loss, fear that God won't meet our needs or give us what we want, all lead to idolatry.

When we don't believe God is who He says He is, we mistrust His heart for us. To walk our own way is rebellion.

Ask the Holy Spirit to deal with the lie that God won't or can't take care of you or the fear that His love and provision must be earned. Ask Him to expose any lies or traumas surrounding the fear.

Focus

The actual focus of a life is the sum total of one's time, thoughts, energy and money. Is anything dividing your heart? Addictions are obvious. Less obvious are the idols of family, ministry, image, beauty, good works, responsibility and even pain.

- Family, though important, should never interfere with our obedience to God. For example, it is a parent's responsibility to raise their children to walk with God. It is not the parent's job to please their children or give them what everyone else has.

- Good works, ministry and responsibility can become an image or identity that we need to feel valuable or important.

- Pain becomes an idol when we judge God for not doing things our way. We put ourselves in the position of Judge, rejecting His redemption of our pain and loss. We view God as a taker, focus on offense and rehearse how He hurt us.

Exchanges

When we worship God, we exchange our weakness for His strength. We exchange our idols for His provision. We exchange our sin for His righteousness!

In a sense, worship is transactional. In worship, we anchor ourselves to the Source for everything in life. Worship acknowledges who He is, and what we are not. We purposely confront ourselves with the character of God and align our hearts to depend on Him.

Anywhere else we seek belonging, comfort, protection, provision or identity other than from God, we have exchanged light for darkness.

- I love my husband's company. If I need him in order to have peace, I've made my spouse an idol. That doesn't mean I should leave my husband, but I do need to adjust my heart.

- If I find my sense of belonging from a club, or church or social group in order to feel okay, it's an idol. It doesn't make those organizations bad, it just means my heart is divided and I'm not experiencing belonging with my Father.

- If peace depends on a person or circumstance, I've exchanged the Peace of Christ for an earthly comfort.

- We become what other people want in exchange for acceptance.

- We give money to charity in exchange for public image.

- We look to a fan club or social group for belonging.

- We serve on a political action committee for significance.

- A career can be a source of pride and identity.
- We look to relationships to make us "somebody."
- A brand promises beauty, popularity or manhood.
- Cars become status symbols. Fashion, homes and the 'right' connections show wealth and success.

The whole world of advertising baits us to make a trade. Every bargain with the enemy is a bad one. We always come out the loser. The inability to let go of that substitute or a lack of peace when we don't have it, reveals an idolatry.

This lack of peace is an invitation to experience God's abundance, nurture and healing.

"I wake up every day worried about my health." Natalie (not her real name) set her coffee down and shifted in her chair. She admitted that God had been prompting her to give up sugar. "It's an addiction. An idol. I want to give it up, but why is it so hard?"

"Sugar has become a false comfort in an empty place," I explained. "Whenever there is a need that we haven't asked God to fill, we are driven to substitutes."

"That's so true." Natalie responded, "Holy Spirit, show me what I need."

God answered right away.

"It's family," Natalie said. "I had to move away from family because of a job. Loss of community and a sense of belonging drove my need. I eat for comfort and I crave sweets most when I'm lonely."

"That adds up," I said. "Community is important. Are you willing to allow God to meet that need?"

Natalie nodded. As she sat with the Holy Spirit, I could see her whole countenance come to rest. "He wants to be my place of belonging," she said. "I can't look to family, or friends, or food or anything else. If I don't allow God to fill that need, nothing else will satisfy. When He has that place in my heart, everything else will just be icing on the cake!"

Natalie repented of using food for comfort. She then received God's Father-love into her heart to experience His presence and companionship.

Idolatry holds us hostage. We may feel full momentarily, but our need for the next fix is inevitable.

We will always miss out on true fulfillment when we make an idol out of God's blessings.

Overcomers

When precious metals are heated to a high temperature, dross rises to the surface. Without skimming off these impurities, the value of the metal is compromised. In the same way, trials serve to expose places we have not allowed the Spirit of God to have full reign. We have a choice: Look our flesh square in the face and take it to Jesus, or cover it up and keep going. We cannot be free of pain, trauma, lies and sin by denial or pretend.

The broken mess of our lives is precisely why Jesus died. It may sound godly to "be strong" and "handle it" on our own, but relying on our own strength despises God's offer of redemption.

"Yet in all these things we are more than conquerors *and* gain an overwhelming victory through Him who loved us [so much that He died for us]," (Romans 8:37).

Transformation happens in the heart from where all emotions and behaviors flow. Our emotions are not impurities. Negative emotions simply *reveal* impurities. True repentance identifies the lie that drives our sin, so the dross can be removed by the Holy Spirit. As our heart is purified, our natural response to testing will be righteousness, peace and joy.

"This is just who I am", "I've always been this way", "it's just my personality", or *"God made me like this,"* flies in the face of the work of Christ. God does not make fearful, impatient, angry or easily stressed people any more than He makes alcoholics or homosexuals.

You are not your sin. This false identity keeps us from experiencing the company of God.

If you see yourself as powerless in the face of sin or fear (victim mentality), then these statements might sound familiar:

- *"I will never be as successful as others."*
- *"I don't have what it takes for this life".*
- *"Beggars can't be choosers."*
- *"I'm on my own."*
- *"I have to make my own blessing."*
- *"Whatever can go wrong, will."*
- *"Nothing works out for me."*
- *"Life is too hard."*
- *"Everyone else has it easier than me."*
- *"I've been wounded, I'm damaged goods."*

Only a victim believes they are created without the strength and capacity to be overcomers. This posture denies that godliness is attainable. If that is so, then any sin becomes acceptable and the Kingdom of God is rendered powerless.

Sin is not who we are or how God made us. Rather, Scripture promises, "For His divine power has bestowed on us [absolutely] everything necessary for **[a dynamic spiritual] life and godliness**, through personal knowledge of Him who called us by His own glory and excellence." (2 Peter 1:3, emphasis mine)

As the Holy Spirit leads us into all truth, our ability to endure trials and heal from trauma increases. (Even if you have been terribly wounded, there is provision for you to heal and be whole. However, if you are in an abusive situation, ask Holy Spirit how to set boundaries for your protection! While God calls us to patient endurance, He never calls us to submit to abuse.) If our heart is anchored in the truth that God is for us, then we will live as conquerors, full of confidence and hope. We know that we have what it takes for every situation. We are not alone. He gives us His strength. We are powerful in Christ to defeat any darkness.

As the Apostle Paul wrote, "I can do all things [which He has called me to do] through Him who strengthens and empowers me [to fulfill His purpose- I am self-sufficient in Christ's sufficiency; I am ready for anything and equal to anything through Him who infuses me with inner strength and confident peace]." (Phil. 4:13)

Godliness is, of course, a journey. But no one gets a free pass to stay in sin. "No one who abides in Him [who remains united in fellowship with Him - deliberately, knowingly, and habitually] practices sin. No one who habitually sins has seen

Him or known Him." (1 Jn. 3:6)

God offers redemption from every sin and every fear. He would not call us to live holy lives and not make it possible to do so.

When we say, *"this (sin) is who I am"*, we identify as sinners rather than saints. Jesus conquered every sin. He gives us the power of His Holy Spirit to be transformed into holy people. Sin may be what we occasionally do, but it is not who we are.

"Father, I repent for identifying as a victim. Even though I may have been wronged, You did not make me a victim. You have made me an overcomer! I declare the truth that You took all my sin (name it) on the cross. I may not always get it right, but You have given me Your righteousness. You give me victory over every sin, hardship and trauma. I can do all things through Christ who gives me strength."

Sons or Orphans

God created every person to belong to Him. He created family to mirror the Trinity where deep connection and fellowship is shared by Father, Son and Holy Spirit. God uses healthy families to show orphans unconditional love. Families are meant to establish children in love and security. But no family is perfect.

Everyone has a raging need to belong. If we don't, we try to fit in.

"Fitting in" is an attempt to find acceptance from people. It drives the question,"Who do I need to be so that you love me?" This quest will never help anyone become their true self or find unconditional love. It allows someone other than God to tell us who we are.

There are only two types of people: Sons/daughters and orphans. Sons know the safety of unconditional love. Orphans are always on alert for the approval of others.

Unconditional love births peace and confidence. Children who are raised with unconditional love may still face rejection or criticism, but rejection and criticism doesn't destroy them. A son or daughter who knows belonging remains true to themselves no matter who they are with. They are not chameleons trying to figure out which color their skin should be next.

The post traumatic response of an orphan heart keeps them on high alert. This hyper-vigilance may feel normal because they've never tasted the feeling of coming home to a safe place. Their antennae is always up to sense which way the wind is blowing, what might happen and how to respond to whatever life might throw at them. An orphaned heart knows no rest; it remains on guard or on high alert.

People's love is fickle. It is human. It disappoints. Hurt on hurt causes layers of brokenness; shame, performance, perfectionism, pretend and self-hatred.

Until we heal from an orphan identity, we will never experience belonging anywhere. We have a vacuum in our soul only our Father can fill.

The left side of the following diagram illustrates the heart of a son, and the right side shows the chaos of an orphan. Study it thoughtfully with the Holy Spirit and ask Him where you are operating from brokenness.

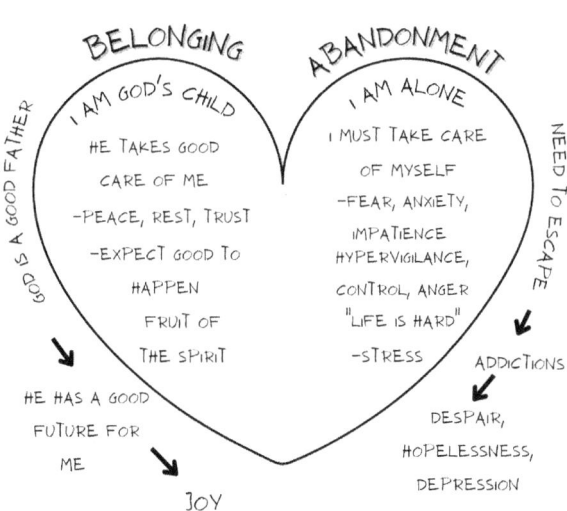

If you recognize the symptoms of an orphan heart, ask Holy Spirit to reveal where you have looked for belonging apart from Him.

Use the following prayers below as a springboard to help you get started. Be specific about people, hurts and your own sin.

Father, I recognize my orphan heart is a result of family hurt. I choose to forgive my family for misrepresenting Your love. I release them from my expectation that they make me feel loved. I need You to re-write what belonging looks like in Your family. Show me how you feel about me.

Father, I repent for seeking belonging apart from You. Cleanse my heart from any sin related to this grasping. I repent for seeking belonging from people, places or groups, careers or personalities. I release them into your hands.

Turn my eyes to You for the love, acceptance and belonging I so desperately need. Place me in healthy relationships with people, so I can enjoy their friendships without looking to them for belonging. I open my heart to You. I need You as my Father. Pour out Your spirit of adoption in me. I need You.

Father God, I forgive the people who abandoned or rejected me. You never abandoned or rejected me. You have chosen me to be Your child. I thank You for your perfect, unconditional love. I repent for believing the lies that I must take care of myself, that I was ever alone, or that You aren't trustworthy. Holy Spirit, come and heal my heart to know the Father's great love. I choose to believe the truth that my Father was always with me, always loving and protecting me. Show me Your Love!

Jesus, I need healing from the poverty of an orphan spirit. Open my heart to receive revelation of Your love for me. Place me in healthy relationships to rebuild my broken childhood into healing and wholeness. I want to be rooted, grounded and established in the Father's love. Pour out on me the spirit of adoption, in Jesus Name.

Trauma

If you continue to feel stuck in your journey, ask Holy Spirit to reveal any unresolved trauma that might be creating walls in your connection to Him. One clue to unresolved trauma is an emotional response disproportionate to the situation.

Missy was our all-black, long-haired German Shepherd. She was a solid 105 pounds of pure marshmallow. You could take food right out of her mouth, and she'd kiss you for it. Missy would even apologize to you if you stepped on her foot. She just loved everybody.

When Allison (not her real name) and her two daughters came to visit, Missy was delighted. She loved children and showered them with gentle affection. Still, Allison would scream and run to hide behind her daughters whenever she saw Missy. Despite an entire evening of Missy's calm friendliness, Allison could not stop displaying violent fear.

Her reaction was completely illogical.

Emotional overreactions are triggered by a replay of events similar to an original trauma. Trauma happens when a person faces a stressful situation beyond their capacity to cope. This sometimes leads to denial of the pain or denial of the event itself. In order to survive significant childhood trauma, we may lock a memory away in a segmented portion of our body or brain. An orange with a worm isolated in one segment illustrates this phenomenon. In people, this acts as a protection for the traumatized. The pain and/or the memories can be totally forgotten until there is time and a safe place to heal.

While this provides a helpful survival tactic for the overwhelmed individual, trauma must eventually be brought to God for spiritual and emotional growth to occur. Otherwise, it remains an area of infection and bondage. Be aware: trauma doesn't have to look significant to have significant impact.

Demons are opportunists who prey on the wounded. The reason Paul tells us to be aware of "the schemes of the enemy" and "put on the full armor of God" is precisely because demons are predators. (Ephesians 6:10-18) They whisper lies ("flaming arrows") into our trauma such as:

- *"God doesn't care about me"*
- *"Something bad could happen at any time"*
- *"Nobody loves me"*
- *"Life is hopeless"*
- *"I have to be strong"*
- *"I have to protect myself"*
- *"I can't trust anyone"*

Lies feel and sound true to a wounded heart.

When words feel and sound true, we usually agree.

The level to which we agree with the enemy's lies determines his level of occupation. A stronghold develops as one lie spreads like the roots of a tree to encompass the mind, thoughts, emotions, will, desires and relationships. A stronghold is a belief system that embraces the mentality and lifestyle of that lie.

Hoarders provide a good example of this principle. A hoarder, not understanding the generosity of Father, has a constant fear of loss or lack. He will likely be stingy, close-fisted, grasping and unwilling to throw things away. He may collect and save newspapers, bread bags and empty cartons of breakfast cereal. Logical reasoning has no effect on a stronghold. Agreements with fear and poverty are soon reflected in the piles of stuff that choke every available space. The spiritual issue manifests in the physical realm.

Trauma shakes our foundational understanding of safety. Lies about God's character grow into the "trauma cracks" of our foundation and expand our sense of insecurity. Strongholds have the power to sway our perspective of reality.

Suddenly, the world is not safe. God is not safe. People aren't safe. Fear and suspicion become our go-to.

Our compass no longer points North.

Trauma can damage our belief in God's love and take us into bondage, or it can drive us into the Father's arms for comfort and truth. With Christ, pain can be a launching pad rather than a place of bondage. The Father's comfort will heal our heart, and Truth will rebuild our foundations.

"And may you, having been [deeply] rooted and [securely] grounded in love... [come] to know [practically, through personal experience] the love of Christ which far surpasses [mere knowledge [without experience] that you may be filled up [throughout your being] to all the fullness of God [so that you may have the richest experience of God's presence in your lives, completely filled and flooded with God Himself]." (Ephesians 3:16-19)

The journey to healing trauma uses the main steps we talked about earlier, with a few steps added. Start with a prayer to ask Holy Spirit for revelation. Remember, He is our guide into all truth. (John 14:15-17, 26)

#1 Identify the emotion. Is this a past trauma being triggered by current events?

Ask yourself: Have I felt this emotion before? Does this present situation feel similar to a past event in my life?

#2 Recognize the connecting trauma.

Sometimes trauma feels too painful and overwhelming to face. Until you address it, it won't stop pursuing you.

Trust that the Father will be gentle and help you face the truth. BUT, if you have deep trauma, seek someone to walk with you through this exercise. Don't try to go it alone!

If you have trouble identifying the link to the past, ask, *Am I afraid of a certain situation that reminds me of the past?* (For example, fear of rejection)

#3 What happened and who do I need to forgive?

Ask Holy Spirit to show you each person involved and specifically what you need to forgive.

#4 What lie did I agree to from my place of pain? What did I believe about myself, God or life because of that trauma?

Helpful questions here could be: *What is my biggest fear in this situation? What does it mean about me if my biggest fear comes true?*

#5 Repent for believing the lies.

Father, I repent for believing the lies that....

Even if you don't see how anything else could be true right now, repent in a posture of trusting that He will give you a new grid to see rightly. As you repent of wrong beliefs, you make space to receive the truth. And the Truth **will** set you free!

#6 Receive God's truth.

Not only do you need to know the truth as facts that Scripture teaches. You need to encounter the reality of who God is and how He was with you in your pain and powerlessness, you need to feel His heart toward you, how He protected you, how was He with you in your pain and how He feels about what happened to you. Go into this question with your imagination open to hearing from the Father.

Healing from trauma is a journey the Father wants to take with us. He cares more about relationship than destination. He desires to experience life with you more than He wants you to get it right. These times of relational connection to our Father are key to growth and healing. Relationship with the Father is what salvation was for. Rules make us slaves, but relationship makes us friends.

It is common in the process of opening your heart to God for healing of trauma, to feel exceptionally raw and vulnerable to the point of re-experiencing the age you were when the wounding occurred. This is a very good sign that you have gotten to the core issues! Give yourself space to allow the "little you" to be; to express emotion, thoughts, memories. Welcome your child; listen to and love those little parts of you. Shepherd that part of your heart into knowing the Savior.

Write down your dialogue with the Holy Spirit. Keep a record of what God says to you and how He shows up to heal your heart. This is a memorial stone. These interchanges with the Father are your weapons to fight with when the enemy throws lies at you. Remember who you are. Remember who He is; bask in His love.

If, in the following days, you see improvement but do not experience complete freedom from a stronghold, there is still an underlying driver (the unholy kind) that needs healing. Continue to ask Holy Spirit to reveal Truth. God can bring deep healing in a moment, but He doesn't always choose to do it that way. God is about relationship and life is a journey with Him. Love heals.

There is a lot that can be written about trauma. We hope that this serves as a starting point in your conversation with the Holy Spirit. Don't hesitate to seek counsel on your journey toward inner healing.

Remember, every one of us is given the Holy Spirit. He is our Healer, Teacher, Comforter, Companion and Guide into all truth.

Besides dealing with root issues, ask the Father to put you into a healthy family if that is foreign to you. Those from broken and dysfunctional families need a new picture (experience) of a loving, godly family to overcome the old one. A new family can help create a new paradigm for receiving God's love. (For examples of how a healthy versus unhealthy family functions, see Appendix B at the end of the book.)

A passage that has been dear to my heart during an extended time of healing is Psalm 84, especially verses 4-7. My prayer is that this will be an encouragement to you as well.

"Blessed *and* greatly favored are those who dwell in Your house *and* Your presence; they will be singing Your praises all the day long. *Selah*. Blessed *and* greatly favored is the man whose strength is in You, in whose heart are the highways *to Zion*. Passing through the Valley of Weeping (Baca), they make it a place of springs; the early rain also covers it with blessings. They go from strength to strength [increasing in victorious power]; *Each of them* appears before God in Zion."

Perfect Peace

When Dwight and I first began to seek God for inner healing, we thought we knew peace. We were fairly stable, even-keeled people. We knew all the verses about peace. We weren't in a panic, we didn't need meds for anxiety. We had peace, right?

But one day, God overwhelmed us with His peace. It wasn't a weekend or holiday. It was a regular day in the presence of the Prince of Peace. It was so far beyond anything we had previously known that it ruined us for the normal.

"Peace I leave with you; My [perfect] peace I give to you; not as the world gives do I give to you. Do not let your hearts be troubled, nor let it be afraid. [Let My perfect peace calm you in every circumstance and give you courage and strength for every challenge.]" (John 14:27)

Whenever we look to something other than God as a source of comfort, distraction, happiness, healing, or life, we abandon the Living Water for broken cisterns. (See Jeremiah 2:13) Broken cisterns constantly need to be refilled. They leak. They leave us needing more as soon as we've had a drink. A fun weekend doesn't fix the daily grind. If anything, going back to reality feels harder.

After having a taste of what God's Peace felt like, we had to have more. Real peace ought to last beyond weekends and fun events. If peace isn't available when life gets messy and hard and stressful, what's the point? Life throws curve balls. The world is full of sin and sinners. I need the Prince of Peace when this world deals out its worst!

Let's face it, sometimes covering up stress feels easier than digging deep! Weekend plans, relentless scrolling, staying busy, eating out, alcohol, entertainment and shopping can all mask our emotional restlessness and pain. But they can't fix the problem.

Jesus said, "Come to Me, all who are weary and heavily burdened [by religious rituals that provide no peace], and I will give you rest [refreshing your souls with salvation]. Take My yoke upon you and learn from Me [following Me as My disciple], for I am gentle and humble in heart, and YOU WILL FIND REST (renewal, blessed quiet) FOR YOUR SOULS. For My yoke is easy [to bear] and My burden is light." (Matthew 11:28-30,)

The Peace of God is remarkably different from what the world calls peace. Take a look at the simple comparative chart below.

World's "peace":

- Can be obtained with medication

- Dependent on good circumstances
- Needs relationships to be conflict-free
- Based on people's approval and acceptance
- Needs life to go according to plan (requires control and manipulation of outcomes)
- Must be able to make sense out of life (can't abide the unknown, mysterious or ambiguous)
- Must have finances in order and plenty of resources
- Needs safety, insurance, bank account, health, good job
- Future must look certain
- Dependent on physical strength, power, title or position

God's Peace:

- Carefree (1 Peter 5:7)
- Restful, without burden (Matthew 11:28-30)
- Without worry or anxiety (Philippians 4:6-7)
- Without fear (Psalm 46:1-3)
- Not shaken by bad news (Psalm 112:6-8)
- Confident in spite of circumstances (Psalm 112:6-8)
- Protects (Psalm 91)

- Thinks on good things (Philippians 4:6-9, Isaiah 26:3, Psalm 131:2, 46:10)

- Sound mind (2 Timothy 1:7)

- Beyond human understanding (Philippians 4:6-7)

- Perfect (Isaiah 26:3)

When Jesus calmed the storm, He commanded the waves, "Peace, be still." Our ability to be still is a litmus test for peace. Stillness is evidence of peace. The inability to be still indicates a lack of peace.

If you want to see how you're doing, take the stillness challenge:

Go outside in nature. No phone, music, headphones or podcasts. Put all life's distractions, situations and relationships in a box and close the lid. "You will keep in perfect *and* constant peace *the one* whose mind is steadfast [that is, committed and focused on You—in both inclination and character], Because he trusts *and* takes refuge in you [with hope and confident expectation]." (Isaiah 26:3)

It will take effort to quiet the mind. That's okay. Practice improves it.

If you can't be in nature, close your eyes and imagine yourself in a favorite quiet place. Relax every muscle. Stop the racing thoughts and self-talk. Sit with the Father.

Listen.

What rises to the surface? The voice of Holy Spirit may be muffled by the noise of your own thoughts. But listen closely. The disquiet (thoughts or emotions) can point out root lies about God. What is the focus of the noisy thoughts? Follow the path to underlying turmoil. Remember, turmoil, restlessness, or feeling "off" are warning lights the Holy Spirit uses to get our attention.

Peace is the result of trust. Any place we lack peace (stillness) indicates a place where we bought into a lie. God's peace is perfect and complete. By recognizing the lies and coming to rest in truth, we find our way back home.

Dashboard Mentality

This book is a way of life. Take your emotional temperature regularly. Check the dashboard and keep asking the hard questions. Put this process on repeat.

Anytime you feel stressed, in turmoil or off-center, ask "Why do I feel this way? What is the lie here? What truth do I need?" Sin falls short of God's glory. Negative emotions indicate places where our lives fall short of understanding His goodness for us. This isn't meant to condemn, but to draw us into abundant life. God has something better.

Yes, that negative emotion may be the cultural norm, but that doesn't make it right or healthy. God didn't mean for you to live with dread. Or shame. Or contempt. Or failure. That list of negative emotions is meant to reveal what should *not* be part of your life.

Matthew 6:22-24 says, "The eye is the lamp of the body; so if your eye is clear [spiritually perceptive], your whole body will be full of light [benefitting from God's precepts]. But if your eye is bad [spiritually blind], your whole body will be full of darkness [devoid of God's precepts]. So if the [very] light inside you [your inner self, your heart, your conscience] is darkness, how great and terrible is that darkness! No one can serve two masters; for either he will hate the one and love the other, or he will be devoted to the one and despise the other..."

This perfectly describes a heart with divided devotion. We may love God, but we align with certain lies and the result is sin we can't seem to shake. It causes confusion and doubt. (See also James 1:8) Truth and lies will never live together in peace.

Until we bring our whole self; mind, thoughts, will, desires, emotions, relationships, into Truth we can't know the perfect peace of God.

You won't regret the peace found in wholeness and freedom. There is much more peace and life waiting for you than you could ever dream.

"But He knows the way that I take [and He pays attention to it]. When He has tried me, I will come forth as [refined] gold [pure and luminous]." Job 23:10

APPENDIX A

Ways to nurture your spirit:

Solitude

Quiet

Fasting

Prayer and Worship (Proverbs 14:27)

Meditation (Psalm 143:5-9; Phil. 4:8)

God's Word and His promises (Proverbs 3:2,7-8)

Soak in His Presence, listen for His voice

Fresh air and sunshine, the sound of water

Beauty (art, music, story)

Share your heart with a close friend

Remember God's miracles, He can do them again!

Walk barefoot, lay on the ground, climb a tree, roll down a hill, swim in a creek, interact with nature/animals

Get your hands in the dirt, smell the soil and the rain, swim in the creek

Pay attention to God's creation and beauty

Mealtimes with family

Laughter

Testimonies (Rev. 12:11)

Eye contact

Love yourself and care for your body

Declare blessings over yourself

For fun: Choose one truth that you have learned from this study and on a sheet of paper, use colored pencils, markers, pens, or paint and brush to be creative with it. Use your artistic genius or the child in you to have fun expressing yourself.

Options: write a verse, a story or poem, draw a picture, splash abstract colors about, put together a collage, or mixed media. Know that God delights in your creation!

APPENDIX B

Healthy Relationships:

- Safe to talk about anything (trust one another)
- Intentionally pursue knowing one another
- Value relationships over tasks, activities, image, stuff or ministry
- Guards and protects one another
- Honors one another, even in conflict or disagreement
- Earns trust with each other
- Consistent in expectations, rules and behavior
- Expect one another to display fruit of the Spirit
- Serve one another, work together as a team
- Communicate needs, wants, and work through con-

flict respectfully

- Apologize and forgive one another
- Consistently accept and love one another

Unhealthy Relationships:

- Not safe to talk about emotions, opinions or desires
- Neglectful of needs, physical and/or emotional
- Demeans, demoralizes, slanders and gossips
- Name calling, yelling, unproductive arguing, blaming
- Manipulation and control
- Lies and deception, sneaky/hidden behaviors
- Rules always changing, never know what to expect
- Angry, moody, temperamental behaviors
- Trauma drama
- Push me/pull you feelings. "I want to be close/I want away from you"
- Cycles of rejection, acceptance, being special, hated
- Verbal, physical or emotional abuse
- Shame, blame, favoritism, unresolved conflict
- Protects family secrets (such as addictions or abuse)
- Cycles of trauma and drama are the norm

Layers of conversation that indicate depth of relational connection:

- Current events, weather, news, and events; surface level

- Share thoughts, ideas, opinions, and goals; appropriate affection

- Intentional about getting to know one another, asks questions and listens

- Encourage and support one another in pursuit of dreams and goals

- Feelings, emotions, heartache, tears and spiritual journey

- Hopes, dreams, disappointments, needs, and hurts

- Worship in hardship together, pray together and for one another

- Share vulnerable places equally with one another in the journey of wounding and healing

APPENDIX C

Emotive Word List (positive)

Accepted

Adopted

Alive

Authentic

Believed

Belonging

Blessed

Bold

Brave

Capable

Caring

Cheerful

Clear-minded

Confident

Comfortable

Compassion

Daring

Disciplined

Encouraged

Excited

Faithful

Free

Generous

Gentle

Grateful

Helped

Honest

Honored

Hopeful

- Humble
- Joy
- Justice
- Kind
- Light-hearted
- Listened to
- Loved
- Nurtured
- Optimistic
- Patient
- Peace
- Powerful
- Precious
- Protected
- Real
- Respected
- Righteous
- Safe
- Self-control
- Sensitive

Strong

Trusted

Truthful

Unity

Valued

Victorious

Vulnerable (but safe)

Whole

Wonder

Emotive Word List (negative)

Abandoned

Accused

Addicted

Afraid

Alone

Angry

Arrogant

Anxious

Betrayed

Bitter

Blamed

Broken

Chaos

Condemned

Confused

Controlled

Cursed

Death

Deception

Demanding

Depressed

Despair

Destructive

Disappointment

Dread

Domination

Entitled

Envy

Escape

Favoritism

Fear

Flattered

Frustrated

Guilt

Hatred/ Self-hatred

Heavy

Helpless

Hopeless

Hyper-vigilant

Intimidated

Invisible

Jealous

Judgment

Lazy

Lonely

Lost

Malice

Manipulated

Misunderstood

Mocked

Neglected

Outcast

Panic

Perfectionism

Perversion

Pity/ Self-pity

Powerless

Prejudice

Preyed on

Pretend

Pride

Rage

Rebellion

Restless

Robbed

Sad

Scapegoat

Selfish

Shame

Silenced

Slandered

Stress

Terror

Threatened

Unloved

Victimized

Violated

Voiceless

Vulnerable (not safe)

Weary

Wicked

Acknowledgments

To my Abba, Father. You are my Healer. Words do not suffice. Writing this book was Your idea, not mine. Bless it in the hands of many for deep healing and restoration to know Your goodness. Take me deeper still. Forever yours....

Dwight, without you this book wouldn't be. Without you I wouldn't be who I am. You gave me space to heal and grow, helped me discover my heart AND you helped edit this book. Thank you!

I am also grateful for the valuable feedback I received from early readers: Emily, Whitney, Tara, Ana and Nicole. Your encouragement kept me going. Thank you!

Please direct all inquieries and correspondence to:

EmotionalDashboard@gmail.com

www.ingramcontent.com/pod-product-compliance
Lightning Source LLC
Chambersburg PA
CBHW060159050426
42446CB00013B/2901